FOUNDATIONS OF MODERN PSYCHOLOGY SERIES
Richard S. Lazarus, Editor

The Psychological Development of the Child,   Paul H. Mussen

Tests and Measurements,   Leona E. Tyler

Motivation and Emotion,   Edward J. Murray

Personality,   Richard S. Lazarus

Clinical Psychology,   Julian B. Rotter

Sensory Psychology,   Conrad G. Mueller

Perception,   Julian E. Hochberg

Learning,   Sarnoff A. Mednick

Language and Thought,   John B. Carroll

Social Psychology,   William W. Lambert and Wallace E. Lambert

Physiological Psychology,   Philip Teitelbaum

Educational Psychology,   Donald Ross Green

The Nature of Psychological Inquiry,   Ray Hyman

Organizational Psychology,   Edgar H. Schein

JULIAN B. ROTTER

Director of the Clinical
Psychology Training Program
University of Connecticut

second edition

Clinical Psychology

71040

PRENTICE-HALL, INC., ENGLEWOOD CLIFFS, NEW JERSEY

Current Printing (last digit)
10   9   8   7   6   5   4   3   2   1

Prentice-Hall International, Inc., London
Prentice-Hall of Australia, Pty. Ltd., Sydney
Prentice-Hall of Canada, Ltd., Toronto
Prentice-Hall of India Private Limited, New Delhi
Prentice-Hall of Japan, Inc., Tokyo

Contents

v

SIX

The Current Status of Clinical Psychology   *106*

WHAT IS THE VALIDITY OF
CURRENT CLINICAL PSYCHOLOGICAL PRACTICE?

HOW EFFECTIVE IS PSYCHOTHERAPY?

THE TRAINING OF CLINICAL PSYCHOLOGISTS

Foundations of
Modern Psychology Series

The tremendous growth and vitality of psychology and its increasing fusion with the social and biological sciences demand a search for new approaches to teaching at the introductory level. We can no longer feel content with the traditional basic course, geared as it usually is to a single text that tries to skim everything, that sacrifices depth for breadth. Psychology has become too diverse for any one man, or few men, to write about with complete authority. The alternative, a book that ignores many essential areas in order to present more comprehensively and effectively a particular aspect or view of psychology, is also insufficient, for in this solution many key areas are simply not communicated to the student at all.

The Foundations of Modern Psychology Series was the first in what has become a growing trend in psychology toward groups of short texts dealing with various basic subjects, each written by an active authority. It was conceived with the idea of providing greater flexibility for instructors teaching general courses than was ordinarily available in the large, encyclopedic textbooks, and greater depth of presentation for individual topics not typically given much space in introductory textbooks.

The earliest volumes appeared in 1963, the lastest not until 1967. Well over one and a quarter million copies, collectively, have been sold, attesting to the widespread use of these books in the teaching of psychology. Individual volumes have been used as supplementary texts, or as *the* text, in various undergraduate courses in psychology, education, public health, and sociology, and clusters of volumes have served as the text in beginning undergraduate courses in general psychology. Groups of volumes have been translated into eight languages, including Dutch, Hebrew, Italian, Japanese, Polish, Portuguese, Spanish, and Swedish.

With wide variation in publication date and type of content, some of the volumes need revision, while others do not. We have left this decision to the individual author who best knows his book in relation to the state of the field. Some will remain unchanged, some will be modestly changed, and still others completely rewritten. In the new series edition, we have also opted for some variation in the length and style of individual books, to reflect the different ways in which they have been used as texts.

There has never been stronger interest in good teaching in our colleges and universities than there is now; and for this the availability of high quality, well-written, and stimulating text materials highlighting the exciting and continuing search for knowledge is a prime prerequisite. This is especially the case in undergraduate courses where large numbers of students must have access to suitable readings. The Foundations of Modern Psychology Series represents our ongoing attempt to provide college teachers with the best textbook materials we can create.

Preface

Clinical psychology is a rapidly growing applied field of the science of psychology. Its primary application is in the field of mental health. The concern with mental health in our society is greatly increasing, and clinical psychologists are being asked to play a major role in solving problems in this field. Yet psychology itself is a relatively new science and its areas of application are in rapid transition. Neither theory nor "facts" are always agreed upon, and in clinical psychology there is no single set of orthodox, approved skills for which a person can be certified as a trained practitioner. A proper description of this area of study must include different points of view. Since the applied techniques cannot stand on their own feet, it is necessary to examine the credibility of the theory and empirical findings on which the various methods of practice rest. The purpose of this volume is to provide an understanding of the nature and present status of the field of clinical psychology. It is intended for beginning students, the intelligent layman, and students of related fields. The book should be of special value to those who wish to consider clinical psychology as a potential occupation.

It is the aim of this book to provide an understanding of clinical psychology on a realistic basis, not glossing over the difficulties, problems, and limitations, but insofar as possible describing its true status and its vast opportunities for development. In trying to achieve this aim the writer has attempted to avoid technical language and dependence upon specialized knowledge of statistics and research methods. The goal is to gain comprehension without resorting to an oversimplification of the complex nature of man or of the problem of understanding him.

Since established theories and methods of application change only gradually, this revision is characterized more by the addition of new material than by rewriting of the previous edition. The volume has been enlarged to include brief descriptions of new developments such as community mental health, behavior therapy, and encounter groups. The revised edition also contains several additional illustrative studies of clinical research, detailing methods as well as findings, and added material to the sections on social learning theory and personality testing.

I am greatly indebted to Dr. Douglas Crowne, Dr. Shirley Jessor, Dr. Richard Jessor, and my wife, Clara, who read the original manuscript and made many helpful suggestions. I should also like to express my appreciation to Mrs. Roberta Markels for her valuable assistance in the preparation of the manuscript. I am also indebted to Mrs. Mary B. Davis for her help in preparing the revised edition.

JULIAN B. ROTTER

What Is Clinical Psychology?

chapter one

Physical scientists, biological scientists, and the educated public increasingly recognize that the solution of technical problems and the conquering of physical disease cannot solve all man's problems of living with himself and with others. The ability to live peacefully, constructively, and happily requires an understanding of man himself. To gain this understanding, many people are turning to the psychological and social sciences, including clinical psychology.

Broadly stated, clinical psychology is the field of application of psychological principles that is primarily concerned with the psychological adjustment of individuals. Psychological adjustment involves problems of happiness—feelings of discomfort, frustration, inadequacy, anxiety, or tension—within an individual, as well as his relationships to other people and the demands, goals, and customs of the broader society in which he lives. Such a definition, however, is a very general one. It does not differentiate clinical psychology from other areas of application within psychology or from many other professional fields also involved in one way or another with the individual's total psychological adjustment.

Within psychology, for example, there are specialties such as vocational counseling, which is concerned with an individual's adjustment to his job; human engineering, which deals in part with man's adjustment to machines;

and school psychology, which involves a person's adjustment to school and learning. Other professions that overlap clinical psychology are those of the psychiatrist,*social worker,* lawyer, speech pathologist, and religious worker. All these professions are concerned in one way or another with the individual's adjustment to a special set of circumstances.

In some cases clinical psychology can be differentiated from other fields in that the latter focus on more specific aspects of adjustment, for example, vocational adjustment or speech pathology. In some instances, though, there is a heavy overlap in interest, as between clinical psychology and psychiatry, both of which deal with broad characteristics of mental illness, or personality disturbance. The difference here lies not so much in application as in the training of practitioners and in the kind of approach to problems. "Kind of approach" refers to the characteristic theoretical orientation that is a part of a particular kind of training. For example, it is characteristic of psychologists to approach mental disturbances as the results of earlier experiences or learning and of psychiatrists to approach many of these disorders as specific diseases requiring specific treatments. Even here, however, there is large overlap between the two fields in their approaches to many problems.

Perhaps we can gain a clearer idea of just what clinical psychology is from looking carefully at what clinical psychologists do. Most of this volume, in fact, will describe what they do, where their ideas come from, and, broadly speaking, how they are trained.

What Do Clinical Psychologists Do?

The activities of clinical psychologists can be divided into three major categories of techniques, or skills. The first of these is the measurement and assessment of intelligence and general abilities. This activity includes not only assessing the present capacity of a person but also estimating his potential, his efficiency, and the effect on his intellectual functioning of the other problems or conditions that surround him.

The second major area of application of clinical skills and techniques has to do with the measurement, description, and assessment of personality, including the diagnosis of what may be termed problem or abnormal or maladjusted behavior. Such diagnostic testing is not merely an attempt to find out what specific disease a person has, as you might find out whether he has measles or chicken pox; rather, it is an effort to describe the individual's psychological condition as thoroughly and as accurately as possible. To make clearer the meaning of personality measurement, or diagnosis,

*This term is defined in the glossary on page 111. Other technical words that appear in the glossary are marked by an asterisk in the text the *first* time they appear.

a brief description of what we mean by personality and personality theories is necessary.

The term personality usually refers to the stable, relatively consistent ways of behaving, thinking, reacting, and experiencing that are characteristic of a particular individual. The term as typically used excludes those stable characteristics of a person that relate to intelligence, achievement, and intellectual skills in general.

Most personality theories are concerned with identifying the most important and most generalized stable characteristics of people and the processes by which they acquire and change these characteristics. If we can measure or identify these characteristics we can understand and predict much of the individual's behavior. Personality theories are also concerned with discovering and describing the experiences, conditions, and events that lead to the development and change of specific personality characteristics and with describing what future behaviors can be predicted from a knowledge of present characteristics. These are the theories clinical psychologists rely on in the development of their tests, diagnostic procedures, and methods of treatment. Personality theories can differ in many ways. Two of the more important of these are *(1)* the emphasis on what aspects of the individual's behavior or total personality are central, and *(2)* views on how these important characteristics develop or are acquired, and how they relate to one another.

The third general area of clinical psychological practice is usually referred to as psychotherapy. To many minds this term applies to a method of treatment wherein a therapist talks to a patient for many hours in an effort to help him understand himself and reach a better adjustment. The term is used here more broadly to describe all the techniques of psychological treatment. These methods include treating patients face to face over a period of time, making recommendations to parents or teachers or directly to the patients themselves, and initiating or making recommendations for changes in the circumstances surrounding institutionalized individuals. In other words, these methods include any techniques or recommendations for improving the adjustment of the individual.

Chapters 3, 4, and 5 will describe these three major functions of clinical psychologists in detail. But you should remember that clinical psychologists may attend to many other things besides these three applied functions. A large number of them teach and carry out research. Sometimes this research is closely related to applied problems, but it may be considerably removed in scope; even so the hope is that such research will eventually lead to a better understanding of clinical problems. Clinical psychologists are also involved in building new or more adequate theories about human nature and with testing these new theories. Although research does not engage all clinical psychologists actively, it is more characteristic of this group than of any other working in the mental health field.

Along with these activities, many clinical psychologists are also interested in other fields of psychology, such as psysiological psychology, experimental psychology, social psychology, industrial psychology, and so on. In fact, the training of most psychologists involves a large common core of basic theory and methodology, so a person who specializes in one or another aspect of psychology usually shares a great deal in training, interests, and activities with colleagues in other branches. To round out the picture of what clinical psychologists do, then, it will be helpful to glance at some of the settings in which clinical psychologists typically work.

In addition to teaching in colleges and universities, clinical psychologists are employed in a great variety of settings. They work in medical schools and university clinics. Perhaps the greatest number of clinical psychologists are currently hired in hospitals for the mentally ill. In such hospitals they not only carry out clinical work and research but also teach, consult with members of other professions, and become involved in personnel selection.* Other clinical psychologists are hired in general hospitals and in adult and child treatment centers. In addition, many school psychologists are trained primarily in clinical psychology.

Clinical psychologists also have important roles in other public institutions, such as schools for the mentally retarded, prisons, reformatories, rehabilitation centers for juvenile delinquents, and establishments for the blind, deaf, and crippled. Industry too has been hiring an increasing number of clinical psychologists to cope with problems of personality selection, counseling, and psychotherapy, and to undertake research on workers' adjustment. Clinical psychologists also do consulting work for government agencies, industry, and other organizations on problems relating to personality measurement, selection, and mental health.

In recent years many clinical psychologists have been involved in what has been called community mental health. This field of application includes a wide variety of approaches and involves many other specialists, such as psychiatrists, sociologists, social workers, and educational psychologists. The main focus of this group is on the community itself rather than specific individuals. Consulting with parents, administrators, and parent organizations in schools, and with religious leaders, business men, and city officials; making job and economic counseling and other needed activities readily available in depressed areas; training people who, with only a minimum of formal professional education, can provide needed psychological services; and helping the members of the community better organize in order to help themselves are some of the activities of these community-oriented psychologists.

Most clinical psychologists work in group settings, usually for the federal government, state governments, universities, colleges, medical schools, or community clinics supported in whole or in part by public funds. Like social workers, they are, to a large extent, in a profession that might be considered to be well on its way to being socialized. Socialized, that is, in that psychologists do not depend for their income on direct payment from individual patients; consequently, their services are available regardless of the patient's ability to pay. A recent survey shows that many clinical psychologists do some individual private work, charging directly for their services, but such private practice tends to account for a relatively small proportion of their time and income. Only a small proportion of clinical psychologists depend on private practice as their main source of income. Although this proportion may be increasing slightly, it is not likely that it will ever equal the proportion of clinical psychologists with public support. In private practice, clinical psychologists may be associated with other clinical psychologists or members of other professions. Their work would include the usual functions of assessment of intellectual abilities, personality diagnosis, and individual and group psychotherapy.

The understanding and treatment of human beings presents many difficult problems. Since many people are unaware of some of their own motives, fail to remember or have difficulty verbalizing their own experiences, and behave differently in different situations, the study of human behavior must involve many complex methods. To describe or treat an individual requires understanding, and the validity of understanding must ultimately be tested by prediction. The following section discusses some of the broad problems involved in the clinician's methods of description and treatment.

Is Clinical Psychology an Art or a Science?

Among clinical practitioners there are those who maintain that the essential judgments in problems of diagnosis and treatment are primarily subjective* ones, based on experience and the individual skill of the practitioner. These clinicians argue that, although the basis for their judgments cannot always be made explicit or obvious, the problems they deal with are so complex that their major tools are insight, subjective discernment, and experience. Such clinicians are arguing, in other words, that there are no hard-and-fast rules to go by, no tests or objective* measures to substitute for the clinician's judgment, and consequently, that the practice of clinical psychology is essentially an art. Some of them argue further that the nature of man is such that it must always remain an art.

Other clinical psychologists, who are sometimes called test-oriented, feel that tests can be scored objectively (that is, in such a manner that anyone scoring them would obtain the same score) and can provide a more accurate and more useful basis for predictions than the judgment of an individual psychologist. They feel that it is increasingly possible to make accurate predictions by such objective means. They argue that clinical psychology is already, to a large extent, a science and can and will increasingly become more so. Before discussing this issue more deeply, though, we should discuss how and why clinical psychologists are involved in problems of predicting human behavior.

When a clinical psychologist makes a judgment about someone's intellectual capacity he does so in order to predict what that person can learn in school or elsewhere and what can be expected of him. When a clinician makes a judgment of how anxious, hostile, insecure, or irrational a person is, he is making a prediction about how that person will behave in a large variety of present and future circumstances. When a clinical psychologist agrees to treat a patient in psychotherapy he is implicitly making a prediction about the potential benefit to the patient; similarly, the way he goes about treating the patient involves, implicitly or explicitly, predictions of how his own behavior will affect the patient. In other words, though he may not say to himself, "I predict that so-and-so will do exactly this under these circumstances," he is almost always making judgments about how the individual will act in other circumstances or how his recommendations, treatment, procedures, and so on, will affect the patient. When he classifies a patient into some category—such as psychotic (insane) or neurotic or delinquent or mentally retarded—he is essentially predicting how the individual will behave in a large variety of circumstances and possibly what kinds of treatment procedures will most benefit him. Even among those clinical psychologists who state that their only concern is understanding, the purpose of this understanding is always to be able to do something to help the patient.

Unless it is argued that there never is a choice in what to do—that is, if it is believed that one should always use the same procedure regardless of how different the patient is—then anyone involved in psychological treatment is likewise deeply involved in problems of prediction. How are these predictions arrived at most effectively? Should we use current tests to the maximum? build more tests? attempt to reduce the judgment of the individual clinician to a minimum so that it could be duplicated by a computing machine, which, given the same information always arrives at the same answer? Or must prediction be left to a more intuitive, more subjective process of individual judgment?

Most clinical psychologists usually rely on what is known as the case method to arrive at both judgments and predictions. So we must examine this method to establish whether, in fact, clinical psychology is an art or a science.

THE CASE METHOD

A clinical psychologist, in arriving at a judgment, compiles as much information as he can within the limitations of time and available sources of data. Some information comes directly from discussion with the clients. It includes their perception of the nature of their problems, the nature of the circumstances in which they live, their feelings, attitudes, desires, goals, and so forth. In addition, in many instances, the clinical psychologist attempts to obtain information from other sources—physicians, teachers, parents, wives, husbands, relatives, and others. He may also obtain data by giving tests to his patient. These may be intelligence tests, tests of special abilities, personality tests, tests presumed to detect brain damage, or special tests of vocational aptitudes and interests. If possible, he attempts to get a developmental (or social) history of his patient so that he can understand how the individual's current attitudes and behavior have developed from specific earlier experiences.

With all patients, whether children or adults, whether mildly disturbed or seriously disturbed, an understanding of the patients' problems requires an understanding of the significant events of their lives. A social history is generally obtained by interview, partly from the client himself and partly from other sources. Some social histories run to several pages in outline form. Obviously, such thoroughness is not possible in every case; consequently, a decision is necessary about what material to obtain and in how much detail.

Although ideally, much of the material is factual—for example, "He was divorced after one year of marriage," or "She failed in the third grade"—facts are only part of a social history. It is not only important to discover, say, that a person was very sick when he was four years old, but also to determine how he and other people felt about his sickness. Did his mother worry that he might die? Was the child himself treated with great concern for many months after his illness? Were the other children jealous of all the attention he got? When the child failed in school later, how did he react? How did his parents feel? What happened to his school work as a result? It is the subjective experiences of the individual that are the focus of the clinician's efforts to understand him. The "facts" obtained are significant as indirect indications of important past psychological experiences.

It is of considerable value to obtain information from various sources because we thereby learn not only "facts" but also how past experiences have been distorted or remembered by various people, including the patient. Such differences themselves reveal how those involved may have felt at the time. For example, in discussing how a child was disciplined in his early years, the mother recalls that the father treated the child harshly. The father recalls that the child had very little discipline and that the mother would "let him get away with anything." An adult patient recalls that her mother was always concerned with her own affairs and with pleasing her husband, but a sister states that the patient was always the mother's favorite and that the mother was always doing things for her. It is not possible for the clinician to discover the "real facts" of one, five, ten, or fifteen years ago, but he does have a further clue to the feelings and experiences of all the participants when he can discover the similarities and differences in their views of the same events.

The importance of obtaining information from many sources, where possible, can also be illustrated by the tendency of different experts to look for, and frequently find, different explanatory "causes." The clinician must be on his guard against accepting any of these as necessarily the basic reasons for a patient's present difficulties. Frequently, the doctor, if asked, will point to some physical condition, the teacher to learning problems, the ophthalmologist to eye difficulties, the parents to mishandling in the school, and the school to mishandling by the parents.

The case method attempts to develop as complete as possible an understanding of an individual and of his past and present interrelations with his social environment. Achieving such an understanding involves integrating information from an individual's present reactions, from his past experiences (as far as they can be determined), and from psychological tests of many kinds with information from other individuals. These data must then be combined in a way that takes them all into account and integrates them —a process that requires great skill and experience.

Having discussed the case method we can now return to the question of whether clinical psychology is an art or a science. Some clinical psychologists, in dealing with adults in psychotherapy, feel that an emphasis on diagnostic procedures, case histories, and information from other sources is detrimental. They limit themselves to attempting to understand only what the patient says in his psychotherapeutic interview. These psychologists tend to emphasize the practice of clinical psychology as an art. Others, who attempt to obtain as much information as possible from tests and other objective sources, in addition to information from the patient or client, tend to emphasize the practice of clinical psychology as a science.

It is abundantly clear at this time, however, that many of a clinical psychologist's more important judgments cannot be made on a purely objective basis. Not only does he lack enough proven rules about what is the correct or most efficient procedure to use in a given instance, but he also often lacks tests and measures of many of the things he considers to be of primary importance in making a judgment. Even when he does have tests, the tests have only limited validity or predictive power.

On the one hand, when assessing personality and intellectual ability, few clinicians would operate without the use of objective tests. On the other hand, it is equally obvious that in the practice of psychotherapy it is not possible for a clinician required to make a judgment to stop suddenly and give the patient a test to decide on the correct thing to do. In short, there is a place in the present-day practice of clinical psychology for both subjective judgment based on experience and skill and for the use of objective tests and objective procedures in general when they have been demonstrated to be useful. For the benefit of the clients themselves it will always be important to try to increase the number and kind of judgments that can be made objectively, thereby eliminating the errors involved in subjective judgment. Nevertheless, it is unmistakable that for a long time to come most of the important decisions of clinical psychologists will be partially based on just such subjective judgment. This is precisely why clinical psychologists, who frequently make judgments that seriously affect other peoples lives, should get the best quality training possible, and why they initially practice under supervision until they have acquired sufficient skill and experience to operate independently. Although not all members of the profession agree, a great many now feel that the Ph.D. degree obtained at institutions whose training programs have been officially approved by the American Psychological Association should be the minimum requirement for practicing clinical psychology. Many clinical psychologists without the Ph.D. degree may well be better clinicians than some with it because of their experience, natural aptitude, or personal assets. Yet where such people take responsibility for important decisions about other individuals, it can be argued that they too would be more effective with more training.

Most psychologists approach the problem of understanding human nature from a scientific point of view. They regard man's behavior as being determined by discoverable natural laws. This scientific viewpoint is sometimes misunderstood by others who feel that the psychologist regards man as a simple machine and so has robbed him of his essential human qualities. In trying to understand man from a scientific or naturalistic viewpoint, most clinical psychologists recognize that man is an extremely complex organism, capable of changing his behavior on the basis of his own thoughts, of creating new ideas and behaviors, and of marvelously intricate and obscure reactions and thoughts. Yet however complex man is, the study of him and of the laws that govern his behavior is a science. Clinical psychology is one of the sciences involved in the study of man. If the efforts of clinical psychologists are going to be effective in increasing knowledge, their methods must conform to the general methodology of science. In applying what is now known to the prediction of an individual's future behavior or to techniques for changing his behavior, it is still necessary for subjective judgment *based upon experience* to play a heavy role. In this sense *only,* clinical psychology is an art as well as a science. This statement, however, does not imply that it is a necessary aspect of clinical psychology, that the discipline cannot become increasingly objective, or that the principles involved in the application of psychological laws to human beings in complex social situations are mysterious and basically not amenable to scientific analysis. Rather, the work of the clinical psychologist must be added to the efforts of other scientists to increase our knowledge of human behavior.

Some Case Illustrations

It will help in understanding the basic nature of the psychological approach to consider three brief case histories. All three cases are boys in the seventh grade who will be called John, Philip, and Ross. All three boys were referred to a psychological clinic for the same reasons: They had stolen money in school and eventually had been discovered. Let us consider the case of John first.

JOHN

The theft.   Asked why he had taken the money from his teacher's purse, John spoke rather bitterly about the teacher, saying that twice she had reprimanded him during the day for speaking out of turn and that toward the end of that same afternoon she had sent him down to the principal's office for talking back to her. What did he do with the money? After taking it, John was worried about being caught and decided the safest thing was to throw the money away in the bushes near school. He said that he himself had no need for the money because he had a generous allowance from his father—five dollars a week—which he could spend in any way he wished.

John's background.   From talking to John and his parents, several important characteristics of his past history were found. John was an only child of a family that lived in one of the better suburbs of town. His father owned his own business and was well-to-do financially, but he spent much time either at work or in his study at home concentrating on his business affairs. He seemed to have isolated himself from his family several years earlier; he now spent very little time in group activities with his family but was generous to them in regard to their physical needs. It was apparent that the father felt somewhat guilty about neglecting John and would give John almost any material thing that he demanded. The father took no part in disciplining the boy, saying that was his wife's job. John's mother, a submissive, somewhat timid, apparently nervous person, expressed a feeling of great inadequacy in her ability to deal with her son. John had never been seriously punished in his life; when he became angry from being frustrated or blocked in something he wanted to do, his mother generally gave in. Although she was very concerned about John and recognized that he was "willful," she felt almost total inadequacy about knowing what to do or how to "handle" him.

John had been going to summer camps since he was five years old. His mother expressed some guilt about the relief she felt while he was gone, but at the same time added that her life was somewhat lonely during these periods.

Psychological tests indicated that John was a boy of somewhat better-than-average intelligence. However, his grades in school had been quite variable. Sometimes he would do excellent work but at other times very poor work, and most of his teachers felt that he did not obtain the grades of which he was capable. Although he knew that stealing was wrong and was afraid of the consequences of being caught, he felt he was right in getting back at the teacher whom he described as mean and unfair. When asked to describe her meanness and unfairness, all his illustrations turned out to be instances in which the teacher simply demanded that he accept the same discipline and classroom rules as the other students.

PHILIP

The theft.   Philip readily admitted taking the money from the lunch room when no one was around. When asked why he took it, he simply said that he needed the money to buy candy, some of which he ate himself, but most of which he gave to younger children in his neighborhood. He expressed no anger toward the school, was sorry that he took the money, but felt that he needed it and that the school would not miss it. He seemed anxious to talk to the psychologist, was eager to please him, and agreed that what he had done was wrong, but supplied no explanation of why he did it other than to buy the candy.

Philip's background.   Philip was a year older than most children in his grade, for he had been kept back once, in the second grade. Since that time he had been promoted regularly, generally with minimum passing grades, but his school work was well below the average of the class. Philip lived in a lower-middle-class neighborhood. His father, a railroad worker, who was away from home much of the time, was considerably older than most parents of children Philip's age, for Philip had been born late in his parents' married life. Philip had two older sisters; one had finished high school and was working, the other had married and left the home. He saw relatively little of either sister.

Philip had always shown some tendency to be heavier than other children, but since the third grade he had become increasingly overweight. From about the fourth or fifth grade on, he had been teased by the other children and called "Fatty." He avoided taking part in athletic activities with boys his own age because he was frequently laughed at, and he had no friends among the boys of his own age group. His only friends were children from his neighborhood who were several years younger, and it was these children he supplied with candy and other gifts when he could obtain them.

Both parents expressed concern for, affection for, and interest in Philip. Both admitted, however, that they felt many of his problems were related to his coming "as a surprise"—that is, he was not a planned-for child, being born when his mother was forty and his father forty-four. The father gave his age and his occupation as reasons for not being able to spend much time with Philip, and the mother excused herself because of her age and health. They had tried to get Philip to cut down on his eating of sweets, to participate more in athletic activities, and to play with boys his own age, but had given up, taking the path of least resistance.

When tested with the Stanford-Binet Intelligence Test, Philip was found to have below-average ability. Although he had never been a behavior problem in school, no teacher had ever taken a special interest in him, and for Philip school was a bore and sometimes a painful experience (when he was called upon to recite, or at examination times when his poor scholastic ability became most obvious). He was, in fact, a sensitive, lonely boy who had few satisfactions in life other than the sweets he ate and the younger children with whom he played

ROSS

The theft.   Ross had also taken money from his teacher's handbag when she was out of the room. When Ross was discovered, he denied that he had taken the money, only admitting the theft very reluctantly when faced with the evidence that others had seen him at the teacher's purse. He was at first quite hostile to the psychologist interviewing him, tried hard to cover up his fear of the consequences, and would give little or no information about himself. When asked why he took the money he merely shrugged. When asked what he did with it, he would only say, "I spent it, I can't remember what I spent it for."

Ross's background.   Unlike either John or Philip, Ross was a popular boy, at least among a large group in the class. Ross's school was in a slum area and most of the children there were relatively poor. Ross was good-looking, athletic, and fond of appearing tough. He was the oldest of three boys, and was looked up to by his two younger siblings. When asked about his brothers, he became protective and showed obvious interest in their welfare. When Ross was about nine, his father had deserted his mother and left town. His mother had obtained a position as a waitress and moved to a small apartment in a poorer section of town. The home itself was physically inadequate, a place to leave with relief rather than return to with pleasure. The maternal grandmother, who was quite elderly, moved in to "take care of the boys." Ross's mother, married early and still quite young, had numerous "boyfriends" but had not remarried. Ross would not talk about his father, and his mother would only say that the father was "no good," "drank heavily," and was frequently out of a job.

Delinquency was a common problem in this school and it seems that Ross was a leader among his age group. Although he had never been caught at a serious delinquency offense before, he had been sent to the principal's office many times for disciplinary reasons, including truancy.

When the psychologist was able to gain Ross's confidence and get him to talk more freely, Ross showed little guilt about taking the teacher's money but some satisfaction that many of the other kids in the class admired him for it and that he would have gotten away with it were it not for the few squares in the class who "squealed on him."

Tests indicated Ross to be of average intellectual ability. Although his school grades were poor, he showed no concern about them and expressed confidence in being able to do what he wanted to do. In general, he did not express hostility or anger toward his teachers, saying that most of them were all right but objecting to a couple who were "too strict." Several times when he was brought to the principal's office the complaint against him was fighting. It turned out that he was protecting his younger brothers, of whom he was quite fond. Apparently he had little respect for his grandmother, but was obviously strongly attached to his mother and would make only positive statements about her.

Ross's mother expressed great worry about him, saying that she could not take care of him during the day because of her job. She frequently returned to the claim that her husband who had deserted her was the reason for all her difficulty. She said that she did not herself have any problem with Ross; he was a good boy at home, and "all his troubles seemed to be at school." Although she seemed to be saying, "It's the school's problem, not mine," once or twice she expressed anxiety about Ross's future.

TREATMENT

It can readily be seen from the three brief case histories above that although these three boys had all committed the same act, they were very different kinds of individuals. In order to understand what they had done and why they had done it, we would have to look into their histories, their backgrounds, and the circumstances surrounding the act. We could not expect either to understand the children and the reasons for their behavior, or to determine how to help them, without knowing a great deal about their histories or past experiences.

To oversimplify greatly, we could say that John had stolen because he was angry and wanted to get back at the teacher who had frustrated and disciplined him. In the past when blocked he had found he could get his way by becoming angry at his mother. In contrast, Philip had stolen because he wanted the money to obtain the only satisfactions that he had in his life, sweets and the affection of the younger children in his neighborhood. Ross in turn had stolen because he expected to obtain the other children's admiration and thus to maintain his status as a leader in a group of delinquent children. In the social environment in which John and Philip lived, stealing was bad and something of which one should be ashamed. In Ross's social environment, stealing was rather a skill and something to be proud of, particularly if one could carry out the act without being caught.

In the treatment of John, it was necessary to spend some time talking with his father. Although the latter was originally very reluctant to come in and take the time away from his business, he later recognized the need. After expressing some of his feelings about his wife and son, he was able to accept his own role of father and parent by attempting to do more things with his son and by providing for him both more discipline and more interest. To a large extent, John's successful treatment depended on the willingness and ability of the father to provide his son with affection and guidance and of the mother to surmount her own difficulties.

In Philip's case, it seemed advantageous to spend more time directly with Philip. His father's occupation and his mother's age and health were such that it seemed wise to provide him with a therapist to whom he could become attached and by whom he could be helped toward greater self-acceptance. In his case, however, the school itself was a crucial aspect of the treatment. Unless the school could provide him with some feeling of self-worth, of recognition for his abilities, of interest in his problems, it was likely that his problems would persist. Consequently, his treatment involved not only many long interviews directly with a clinical psychologist aimed at increasing Philip's self-acceptance, but also several conferences among the teacher and school authorities and the clinical psychologist.

In many ways Ross's treatment was the most difficult. His mother could not give up her job and his grandmother was far too old and too uninterested in him. The very behavior the psychologist sought to change was approved and rewarded by the boy's peers, with whom he spent the most time and from whom he obtained most of his life's satisfactions. Although it is possible that individual treatment of Ross and the cooperation of the school could make some changes, unless major social changes were made in his whole community, the prospects for successful treatment were dim. In fact, serious treatment of Ross was not attempted because of community limitations. The availability and use of boys' clubs and social activities provided by the community, special professional personnel in the schools, and the provision of more adequate low-cost housing would have all been helpful in the successful treatment of Ross.

What these three cases illustrate is that psychology is essentially a historic science. Unlike physics, chemistry, or other physical sciences, in which to explain an event it is necessary only to consider the immediate forces acting in a situation, in order to explain an event in psychology and make predictions about a future one, it is necessary to know the previous experiences of the individuals involved. Many different patients might have the same label—such as mentally retarded, schizophrenic, delinquent, stutterer, neurotic—and they are so labeled because of the similarity of their behavior. But it cannot be assumed that the people with the same label are really very similar, that they can be treated the same way, or that their future behavior can be predicted from their present actions. The *laws* governing the acquisition of new behaviors and the selection of alternative behaviors in complex situations are assumed to be the same for all. Since each individual has a different set of experiences, however, each is a unique case who must be studied in terms of his life history in order to understand him fully.

This latter statement should not be taken to mean that the clinical psychologist or personality theorist should not use categories or general descriptive terms to indicate the similarities among persons. In order to generalize what we learn from one individual to another we must have descriptive dimensions that indicate similarities. Even so, just because a number of individuals may be similar in one dimension (such as homosexuality, low intelligence, or hostility to others) does not mean that they are *types* who are similar in all characteristics. Understanding the behavior of a specific person does not follow from some single label, category, or type into which he has been pigeon-holed, but rather from understanding the complex interaction of many different characteristics.

Historical Trends

chapter two

Clinical psychology is one of the most rapidly changing applied fields within the social sciences. Compared to 1940, the number of clinical psychologists in this country has doubled, redoubled, and is still rapidly increasing. At the same time, the kinds of activities, the kinds of techniques and methods, and the theoretical approaches used have also been undergoing rapid change. To understand the present-day practices in clinical psychology, it would be helpful to see them in light of historical perspective.

In this chapter a brief general overview of influences and changes in the field of clinical psychology as a whole will be presented. In the three chapters that follow, describing the present major functions of clinical psychologists, the specific background for each function will also be noted.

Early Beginnings of
Clinical Psychological Practice

The tap roots of clinical psychology lie in two fields of study. One of these is the study of abnormal behavior, including mental retardation, or feeblemindedness. Late in the eighteenth century some physicians became interested in abnormal behavior, regarding it for the first time since Hippocrates and Galen as illness rather than as a result of possession by devils, witchcraft, or other mystical causes. The nineteenth century saw several attempts to classify these disorders and, at least in France, crude attempts at treatment. Although some psychologists were involved in these early attempts to describe mental pathology, many of the people involved were trained as physicians. French and German physicians, such as Louis Rostan, Jean Charcot, Emil Kraepelin, and Ernst Kretschmer, and psychologists, such as Pierre Janet, began to describe specific disorders as natural phenomena and sought the etiology of these mental abnormalities. Charcot, Janet, and Hippolyte Bernheim began to treat "hysterics" (persons with serious physical complaints but no observable organic pathology) with hypnosis. In the United States, the interest in handicapped and emotionally disturbed children was taken up by Lightner Witmer, who established the first psychological clinic in 1896 at the University of Pennsylvania. About the same time, William James, the psychologist and philosopher, made lasting contributions to the fields of normal personality and abnormal psychology.

The other general field that nourished clinical psychology was the study of individual differences. The great early figure in this field was an Englishman named Francis Galton. Galton was a scientist whose interests ranged over many fields. In the 1880s his studies of individual differences, particularly of great men, established a field of study that has been an important aspect of American psychology ever since. In 1890, shortly after Galton, an American psychologist James McKeen Catell, who was interested in individual differences, published an important article entitled "Mental Tests and Measurements." Through his work and that of the psychologists who followed him, the development of psychological tests became an important aspect of American psychology.

Test-making was not confined to America, however. In France, Alfred Binet along with Theophile Simon published a rather extensive test for measuring the ability of school children in 1905. Developed at the request of French school authorities, the test was specifically designed to "diagnose" those individuals sufficiently retarded mentally to be unable to benefit from regular school instruction. This test marked the beginning of the use of objective psychological instruments for the diagnosis of mental abnormality. Originally known as the Binet-Simon Intelligence Scale, it has been revised many times and is still the fundamental test in use in this country for the assessment of the intelligence of children. It is currently titled "Revised Stanford-Binet Intelligence Test."

General Trends in Modern Clinical Psychology

Before World War II most clinical psychologists worked primarily with children's problems. They did so in settings such as university clinics, community clinics, traveling clinics operated by state departments of public welfare and sometimes by state departments of education, institutions for the feebleminded, clinics for the physically handicapped, speech pathology clinics, and institutions for delinquent children. Their major job was to give psychological tests, which dealt primarily with intellectual ability and school achievement, and with special aptitudes (such as those for mechanics and music) and special disabilities (such as difficulties in language, memory, and auditory and visual perception).

Along with the data obtained from these tests, case studies were obtained either directly by the clinical psychologists or from information provided by social workers or teachers. The assembled facts were used primarily to make recommendations, usually to teachers, parents, and therapists involved in special handicap training (teachers of speech correction, teachers of the deaf, the blind, and so on). Recommendations were also made to physicians, to the authorities of juvenile institutions, to the courts, and to other social agencies.

The university training of these clinical psychologists, which was directly related to their clinical work, was generally quite limited and usually included only a course on the administration of the Stanford-Binet Intelligence Test, a course on group testing, one on abnormal psychology, and possibly one on child psychology or child development. Most of their training took place on the job as field experience. In a few rare instances there were genuine internships such as the one at Worcester State Hospital described by David Shakow in 1938.

Rarely did the clinical psychologist do extensive face-to-face psychotherapy with children. When such therapy was done, usually in community clinics, the methods used were based on descriptions of therapy through play developed by Anna Freud and Melanie Klein, who applied Sigmund Freud's psychoanalytic methods to psychotherapy with children. Occasionally, a common-sense kind of psychotherapy was carried out by clinical psychologists working with adolescent delinquents and with persons who had speech problems, particularly stutterers.

Work with adults was distinctly less common than work with children. Primarily, clinical psychologists working with adults had some institutional placement, usually within a state psychiatric hospital, in which their primary job was to give tests to aid psychiatrists in making diagnoses. Other available positions were in prison systems where the psychologists tested for intelligence, tried to determine which inmates were mentally ill, and gave special tests to help in placing convicts in prison jobs and schools. Prison psychologists occasionally did individual or group pyschotherapy. In psychiatric hospitals, however, individual and group psychotherapy tended to be rare, and, if present at all, represented only a minor aspect of the job of the psychologist. Clinical psychologists in institutional positions frequently found themselves involved in problems of hiring or selecting attendants, aides, or other personnel. Their function was to give tests to applicants and to evaluate intelligence and personality adjustment or emotional stability.

Toward the later thirties, emphasis on personality testing, particularly with adults in mental hospitals, began to increase, but it was still heavily outweighed by the emphasis on tests of ability and defiency, tests purporting to determine loss of mental ability resulting from mental illness or brain damage, and tests of special skills and disabilities. Most books published in this period in the general area of clinical psychology provided descriptions of how to give, score, and interpret mental tests. Most research of clinical psychologists dealt with the diagnostic value of tests of intellectual functioning or the development and validation of new diagnostic tests. Psychologists rarely were involved in the publication of descriptions of methods of face-to-face treatment.

The advent of World War II, the war itself, and its aftermath, all produced important changes in the practices of clinical psychologists. One of the important early effects of the political upheaval in Europe in the late thirties was a large migration of European psychologists and psychiatrists to the United States to escape the totalitarian regimes. Many of this group had psychoanalytic interests and training. Although they did not initiate psychoanalytic thinking in this country, their activities and writings led to an increased interest in personality and personality development in general and psychoanalytic concepts in particular. The general effect on the clinical psychologists and psychiatrists with whom the newcomers came in contact was to reduce the emphasis on testing intelligence, deficits, and abilities and to increase the emphasis on personality and the measurement of deviant personality characteristics.

The war itself led to an increased interest in clinical psychology and in the potential contribution of clinical psychologists to the treatment of mental patients. The large number of rejections in the draft for reasons of emotional instability and intellectual deficiency and the number of psychological casualties in the armed forces led to a greater national concern with the general problem of treatment and prevention of mental disorders. This attitude was reflected in a greatly enlarged budget for the National Institute of Mental Health following the war. Psychologists made a strong impression on people working in the mental health field, not only because of their techniques, which could be used for selection, but because of their general knowledge of research methods. During the postwar period the United States Public Health Service, in making grants to the states for mental health purposes, placed great stress upon hiring clinical psychologists, for both clinical and research purposes.

Within the armed forces a large number of psychological breakdowns, preceding or during combat, found the medical services inadequately equipped to deal with the problem. Psychiatrists were few in number; consequently both psychiatrists and clinical psychologists were trained in short courses to deal with the problem. Again the psychologist, with his selection techniques and his knowledge of research methods, created a strong impression on the people working in this field. The plans for an expanded program for the care and treatment of veterans included substantial sums for the training and hiring of clinical psychologists.

Support for training of clinical psychologists, both from the United States Public Health Service and from the Veterans Administration, went to those universities that undertook extensive programs at the Ph.D. level. Many of the students themselves were supported by working in the Veterans Administration facilities that were scattered throughout the states. These students had, as their clinical population, adults who had been psychologically incapacitated to some extent by their army experience. Since the Veterans Administration training program was the largest in scale, a major trend after the war was increasing interest in the personality problems of adults. The Veterans Administration itself was willing to hire the psychologists who finished in approved programs at salaries generally exceeding those that could be obtained in schools, prisons, or community centers. Consequently, a marked increase in interest and training for working with adults with personality breakdowns or problems ensued in the postwar period.

During the war, the practical necessity of returning as many men as possible to combat led to a number of expedient attempts to give psychotherapy to patients. When clinical psychologists were available, they were frequently pressed into providing group psychotherapy and, in some cases, individual therapy.

During and immediately after the war, the work of Carl Rogers in the field of psychotherapy, particularly his emphasis on publishing exact transcriptions of therapy sessions, created widespread interest. The somewhat sterile approach to classification and labeling of mental disorders yielded, at least for many psychologists, to a strong desire to undertake therapy, to do something that would be immediately helpful to the patient. This interest in adult psychotherapy and the presence of lay and medically trained analysts from the continent, opened up for clinical psychologists the area of long-term, face-to-face treatment of adults. This practice had previously been the almost exclusive domain of a few psychoanalytically trained psychiatrists. That one had neither to be psychoanalyzed, nor to be psychoanalytically oriented, nor to have an M.D. in order to offer treatment, became readily accepted by clinical psychologists.

The United States Public Health Service supported a conference on the training of clinical psychologists at Boulder, Colorado, in 1949. This conference resulted in a number of general agreements, one of which was to try to make the Doctor of Philosophy degree a minimum requirement for an individual calling himself a clinical psychologist. Thus, not only in universities, but in many practical settings, clinical psychologists were formally or informally required to have the Ph.D. Many universities even gave up training clinical psychologists below the Ph.D. level. Due to the large number of openings now available, it was natural that most clinical psychologists, with their greater investment in training, would enter the positions with the best economic future. Since these did not include community clinics, prison systems, school systems, clinics for the physically handicapped, and so on, a general drift began toward work with adults and adult problems. More and more clinical psychologists accepted positions in the Veterans Administration, state hospitals, universities, university medical schools, private practice, and in industrial consulting firms. By 1960, however, the problem of treating veterans had become less acute and interest in child treatment and child problems began once more to increase.

It is interesting to note these changes since they illustrate how social, economic, and political events affect the direction of development of a science. The kinds of problems investigated and the way they are conceived are generally heavily influenced by the conditions in a society, not independent of them. New directions in science, besides influencing the nature of future changes, arise from changes that have taken place in a society.

Summary

The beginnings of clinical psychology lay in the work of French and German psychologists and physicians in the classification of mental abnormalities, and in the study of individual differences, primarily in England and the United States. Early clinical psychological practice was concerned with the devising and giving of individual mental tests for diagnostic purposes.

Since the early thirties, a general shift in the interests and activities of clinical psychologists has taken place *(1)* away from a major emphasis on children's problems and handicaps to problems of adult adjustment, *(2)* away from a strong emphasis on intelligence testing and testing for psychological deficits and interference in intellectual functioning to an interest in testing for personality description and adjustment, and *(3)* away from an interest in the classification of mental abnormalities with an emphasis on the psychologist's function as a tester to an interest in psychotherapy and the actual management of cases.

The Measurement of Intelligence and Abilities

chapter three

What Is Intelligence?

There are many different definitions and many different interpretations of
the concept of intelligence. The view most widespread among nonpsycholo-
gists is that intelligence is a person's general inherited, relatively constant
capacity to learn, solve problems, and adjust to his environment. Many
aspects of this definition have been seriously challenged, however. How
general is this potential? To what extent is it really constant? To what extent
is it determined by genetic factors, to what extent by intrauterine and
physical conditions of early infancy? To what extent is it determined by
training, stimulation, environment? Does the notion of intelligence represent merely an average of many specific abilities or is it truly some general
capacity that in turn affects the learning of other more specific skills or
abilities? If a student does well in arithmetic does that mean he *should* be
able to do equally well in French? If he has a good vocabulary should he
be able to learn mechanical things easily?

There has been, and still is, much confusion in the attempts made to
answer these questions, partly because many people who ask the questions
misunderstand the nature of psychological terms, concepts, or constructs.

Even the beginning student in psychology is unlikely to have a real under-standing of the nature of psychology as a science, unless he understands the nature of scientific terms as used in psychology.

The Nature of Psychological Constructs

If a series of common household objects were arranged in a room and you were asked to describe them, you could draw on a series of descriptive terms ranging from very general to very specific, depending on the number of objects to which each term could be applied. For example, the term heavy could be used to describe some of the objects but not all, whereas the property of weight could be ascribed to all the objects. The concept of weight, that is, is more general than the concept of heavy or light. The terms heavy or light, in addition, are *relative* terms; they are not absolute proper-ties of objects, but have meaning only in relation to other objects. Is a chair heavy or light? If we call a chair light does that mean that we may not call heavy any object that weighs less than the chair?

Similarly, blue might describe some of the objects present but colored will apply to them all. Color is a more general concept than blue. But where is the color in the object? Where is the blue in the sky? Where is the height in the table? Where is the roundness in a ball? What we are trying to illustrate with these questions is that the terms used to describe the events of nature deal with *aspects* of events, not with the events themselves. They need not have any specific locus in the objects they are describing, nor any absolute meaning. *A concept, construct, or scientific term is an abstraction of some aspect of an event made from a particular point of view.* Constructs range from specific to very general and serve various purposes for the people who use them.

Now suppose you took a number of machines—some in poor working order, some in working condition but with obvious difficulties, and some in smooth working order—and asked someone to describe the working condi-tions of these motors. He might say that they were all inhabited by gremlins. In the motors that are working well, the gremlins are asleep. In those that are working poorly, the gremlins are up and beginning to make trouble. And in the ones that are not working at all, the gremlins have made the machine break down. Now, if you ask this individual, "How do you know when the gremlins are sleeping and when they are not?" or "When are the gremlins causing the motor not to work and when is the fault with other things, like broken parts or lack of fuel?" he may tell you that when he can find none of the other things, the trouble is always being caused by gremlins.

This example illustrates two things about concepts, terms, and con-structs. One is that just because someone uses a term does not necessarily mean that this term mirrors something that is real. The other is that a concept, whether "real" or not, may serve the purpose for a person of accounting for what he cannot otherwise explain. In this instance, however, the concept would be wholly unsatisfying to a scientist or mechanic, since it does not tell how to fix a machine or when to expect it to work and when to expect it not to work. The gremlin construct may be useful to one person for a particular purpose but not be useful at all to the scientist who is interested in predicting events or understanding how they come to be.

In all sciences terms that have been used at one time to describe the events of nature have later been discarded as poor or erroneous conceptions. The belief that a term of long standing is necessarily accurate or scientifically useful is mistaken. Practitioners of the more advanced sciences have learned to ask the question "What is the most predictive or useful way of describing some events?" rather than "What is this thing really?" Psychology, being a relatively new science, has many terms and concepts that require revision or elimination and eventual replacement by better ones. The modern scientist does not ask the question "What is intelligence really?" He rather asks, "What is a useful way of describing people's abilities so that we can best understand why they behave the way they do and what may be anticipated about their future behavior?"

For the scientist there are two characteristics of scientific terms themselves that can be used as criteria for their value. One of these is *reliability* or measurability. By reliability we mean the degree to which the same event, observed by many different scientists, would be described in the same way by all of them. Obviously, if a group of scientists observing the same event came up with very different measures for the same variable, communication would be limited and there could be no body of public knowledge. If the terms and concepts used by scientists are not reliable, there is no science in the true sense, only the individual subjective opinions of a number of different people.

The other general criterion for a good concept, term, or construct is its *utility* for a given purpose. We cannot look somewhere into an object to find out whether its weight is really there, yet the concept of weight is valuable and useful for many purposes. When we consider the weight of an object, we are able to understand something about the force it exerts when it falls. We can make predictions about how the object will act under many conditions. By taking into account other concepts along with weight, such as size and porosity, we can predict whether it will float. In other words, the utility of a concept can be defined as the degree to which it enables us to understand how some event came to be, what conditions gave rise to the event, and what predictions we can make about the future. As we shall see later, not only is the concept of intelligence as a general, inherited, stable capacity limited in utility, but so also are many concepts developed in earlier times about the nature of abnormal behavior. The question we shall try to answer at the end of this chapter is not What is intelligence, really? or What are the true components of intelligence? Rather, we shall attempt to answer the questions What is a reliable and useful way to describe people so that we can understand why they perform as they do in regard to various skills? and How can we predict their future behavior?

Intelligence, Aptitude, and Achievement

Intelligence, aptitude, and achievement are related but distinct constructs that have been relied on heavily in the past. Having briefly examined the nature of constructs in general, we can now evaluate the meaning and adequacy of these concepts.

Although intelligence is usually regarded as a very broad capacity, aptitude has been taken to refer to more specific abilities or learning potentials; both are assumed to be stable and genetically based. Thus, one speaks of musical aptitude, mechanical aptitude, athletic aptitude, artistic aptitude, and so on. As distinguished from both of these, achievement is a matter of what an individual has already learned. Thus, there is achievement in mathematics, in reading, in spelling, in knowledge of mechanical principles, and so forth. It is assumed that some individuals, through great effort, can achieve a higher level of performance than might be predicted from their general ability or intelligence; conversely, some may achieve much less than they might have because of low motivation or emotional problems.

In fact, many tests presumably measuring different things utilize some of the same items, and they *all* measure what the test-taker has already learned. The differences, if there are differences, lie in the specific items used or the nature of the items. For example, both intelligence tests and tests of reading achievement measure vocabulary knowledge and the ability to read and understand what has been read. Although the makers of intelligence tests attempt to use items or questions that most people have had an equal opportunity to learn, they cannot always achieve this goal. In fact, intelligence tests reflect past opportunity to learn almost as much as do school achievement tests. Perhaps what differentiates the two is that the former sample many different abilities in order to arrive at some average description, while the achievement and aptitude tests only measure more specific abilities. Scores on intelligence and achievement tests may also differ for an additional reason. Achievement tests are frequently given in groups and intelligence tests individually; varying scores may merely reflect the different motivation and security a child feels in the two situations.

What Is the IQ?

When Binet and Simon developed their test, they tried to find specific problems or tasks or items that most children at a given age could handle.

They then arranged all their entries in age levels, and the score a child obtained on their test was the average age level at which he was functioning. Thus, a particular child could be characterized as passing tests at the average level of a seven-year-old or eight-year-old or a four-year-old. By giving a specific amount of credit for each item, a tester could arrive at averages. For instance, if there were four tests at some particular age level and a child passed two of them, he would be given credit for half a year. For example, at the eight-year level the child might have passed an item requiring him to successfully define ten words from a larger list and an item requiring him to repeat from memory a simple sentence. But he may have failed an item requiring him to point out the absurdities in a series of pictures and one asking him to name the days of the week in order. According to the test, he would be functioning at the level of a seven-and-a-half-year-old, provided he passed all the tests at lower levels and none at still higher levels. To set up a criterion for determining whether a child could benefit from further schooling, Binet arbitrarily selected two years' retardation—that is, two years' lag behind one's chronological age—as an indication of serious retardation. The average score on the test was called the mental age, and the child's actual age, his chronological age.

It soon became apparent that this criterion of two years' retardation had a different meaning at different age levels. For example, an eight-year-old who is two years retarded is clearly more seriously retarded than a fourteen-year-old who is two years behind. That eight-year-old might well be expected to be far more retarded at age fourteen as his lack of skills continues to interfere with his learning of the increasingly complex tests he has to master as he gets older. To give this criterion a more constant meaning at different age levels, Wilhelm Stern suggested the use of an intelligence quotient, to be derived by dividing the mental age by the chronological age, both expressed in total months, and multiplying the quotient by 100, as in the formula below.

$$IQ = \frac{\text{mental age (in months)}}{\text{chronological age (in months)}} \times 100$$

It can be seen from this formula that if the individual's mental age and chronological age were the same, his IQ would be 100. If the tests were constructed so that exactly half the people at a given age level passed any particular item and half failed, then 100 would be an average IQ. In fact, it was a goal of Binet and Simon and other test-makers to achieve just this average score. Later intelligence tests were based on a somewhat different principle—the setting of norms * for each age level. These norms might be derived from the number of items passed or the number of seconds necessary to complete a task or any other scoring standard. The average performance for children of a given age would then arbitrarily be assigned the score of 100, and other IQ scores would be set so that they could be comparable to the Binet IQ, which is based on the relation between mental age and chronological age.

Although there are limitations to a too-general concept of intelligence itself, any particular test of intelligence is perhaps even more limited. Nevertheless, people started taking a person's score on some intelligence tests as a relatively stable characteristic. First psychologists, then teachers, and then laymen began to ask about an individual, What is his IQ?—as if it were some special property that he would carry around with him all his life and that would explain much of his behavior. Instead of merely being the score on some particular test, given under particular conditions, the IQ was treated as a permanent personal attribute. It is probable that this reification * of a test score has created far more harm than good, by leading to a general and widespread misconception of the nature of intellectual function.

For one thing, the concept of intelligence on which the test itself is based may be inadequate, lacking any real predictive value. Second, the test may not be a good test of the abstract concept it is intended to measure—that is, the items may not have been well selected, they may not be appropriate to many people who might take the test, and the norms (or standardizations) may be based on too few people. For example, in one test in the Wechsler intelligence scales the subject is to arrange in order a series of comic strip cartoons in which no language is involved. Such a test favors those who have had experience with reading comic strips in a daily newspaper and penalizes those who have not. In addition, studies demonstrate that, although many intelligence tests correlate or covary with one another, or produce similar scores, there are also great differences among them. There is also evidence that the scores on intelligence tests do change over an individual's lifetime, sometimes quite markedly.

If a first- or second-grade child gets a low score on an intelligence test and does poor schoolwork, it is frequently assumed that he lacks the innate capacity to do any better. As a result, no one looks into the reasons for his poor performance and he is merely accepted as an inferior student who cannot be expected to learn. Yet his bad showing in the first and second grade may be due to a lack of language stimulation at home, his parents' use of another language, his being upset and frightened by the testing experience, his being negativistic when asked questions, or a great many other possible reasons. Indeed, his poor work in school might be just as much a result of neglect by his teachers as of limited learning potential. Of course, a good clinical psychologist would try to assess those factors that interfere with good performance on a particular test, but, in many instances, the people giving tests are undertrained. Often, group tests are given, and the scores are taken just as seriously as those of individual tests, which provide a much greater opportunity to observe all the factors determining a child's performance. In any case, it is abundantly clear that regardless of the test used, ability to do well on an intelligence test, as well as ability to do well in school, varies greatly over the school years. For some individuals this variation may be extreme, for others relatively small.

An extensive 16-year study by Marjorie P. Honzik, Jean W. MacFarlane, and Lucille Allen of the IQ scores of 222 children in Berkeley, California, illustrates the above point very well. These children were first tested at age 21 months and were followed through to age 18, each child getting approximately 10 individual intelligence tests during the period. Marked changes in IQ during the preschool years were typical, and scores during school years, when the tests are presumably more reliable and ability level is assumed to be relatively stable, still showed a great deal of variability.

Table 1 shows the range between the highest and lowest IQ scores of the 222 children during the presumably stable 12 years from 6 to age 18. It can be seen from the table that 9 percent, or 20, of the children varied in their IQ by 30 or more points. Over half of the subjects (58 percent) varied by 15 or *more* points.

Despite such evidence of variability, numerous studies of the predictiveness of the IQ do show that some tests have real value in predicting school grades and certain intellectual problem-solving skills. It will be seen later that measures of intelligence are also useful in determining whether a person is functioning normally. Scores on intelligence tests, however, have frequently been overvalued by the public, who have assigned almost magical properties to the IQ. In fact, what an IQ represents is a score obtained on a given test, on a given day. What can be predicted from it is a matter of hard scientific information. The predictions from any particular test have their limitations and represent the average of many children. For a particular individual they may be highly inaccurate. In any case, the ability to

Table 1

Changes in IQ Scores for 222 Children
Examined Between the Ages of Six and Eighteen

RANGE OF IQ SCORES	PERCENTAGE OF CHILDREN
50 or more IQ points	0.5
30 or more IQ points	8.5
20 or more IQ points	26.0
15 or more IQ points	23.0
10 or more IQ points	27.0
9 or less IQ points	15.0

From Marjorie P. Honzik, Jean W. MacFarlane, and Lucille Allen; "The Stability of Mental Test Performance Between Two and Eighteen Years," *Journal of Experimental Education* 17 (1948): 309–24, by permission.

predict future performance from a single score obtained at a particular time has been grossly exaggerated in the minds of most people. As stated earlier, the problem of making a prediction about a complex human being behaving in a complex environment is extremely difficult, requiring information obtained from many sources, and a skilled and experienced clinician to put the information together in a useful manner.

A Modern Conception of the Nature of Intelligence

The evidence for, and utility of, the genetic view of intelligence has been critically examined recently by Shephard Liverant who has sharply attacked the older view of a general, genetically determined intellectual potential.[1] The notion of a more-or-less stable inherited capacity, which the individual may learn to use or may fail to use, is gradually being rejected.

Modern theories of both behavior and genetics are no longer consistent with the simple notion that there is a gene for intelligence that is inherited in some simple Mendelian fashion. Rather, it is generally understood that a large number of genetic factors influence the proper development of the fetus. These influences along with influences of the gestation period in the mother produce persons with differing neurological organization and differing potentials to respond to stimuli. In some cases there may be limitations on what a particular person can learn and in other cases the characteristics of the individual may be such as to facilitate the learning of particular discriminations and the speed of acquisition of new behaviors. There is no question that a child's characteristics at birth influence the development of his intellectual skills, but they do not determine what or how much he will learn, and they may act either positively or negatively on the learning process, depending on the nature of the specific learning experience.

A child may be fast at making auditory discriminations but slow at learning eye–hand coordinations. How can we explain such differences? Actually, at this point, relatively little is known about the physiological characteristics of newborn infants that facilitate learning under particular conditions; we know more about physiological characteristics that interfere with or limit learning under specific conditions. Experience after birth interacts with these initial qualities to produce the acquisition of skills. Serious personality problems, or what is sometimes called emotional factors, and the amount and kind of stimulation are known to be of importance. We still need to learn a great deal about the role of specific periods of

---

[1] "Intelligence: A Concept in Need of Reexamination," *Journal of Consulting Psychology* 24 (1960): 101–110.

development and the importance of particular kinds of experiences at crucial times in the development of skills. In any case, it is unlikely that any individual, whether generally recognized as a creative genius or considered to be hopelessly mentally deficient, ever fulfills as much of his potential as he could if more were known about how to utilize experience and motivation at crucial points in order to obtain an optimum development of skills.

It must also be recognized that what a person can do at any particular time is not only dependent on his past experience and initial equipment, but also on the immediate situation and such variables as his motivation to perform, the degree to which his anxiety or his expectancy for failure interferes with his behavior, and the nature of his social relationships.

Although research shows that there is better than chance correlation of one academic skill with another under particular testing circumstances, there is still a great deal to be learned about the relation of more complex skills to academic ability. For example, there is some evidence that among bright people the ability to memorize is not highly correlated with the ability to be original. Likewise, the ability to learn other people's motivations or even to predict their behavior may not be highly related to academic skills.

In short, the traditional construct of intelligence needs to be drastically revised or to be supplanted by better descriptions of ability. Psychologists now regard complex problem-solving as a series of skills (verbal, mathematical, creative, social, mechanical, and so on) that a person may or may not acquire. Failure to acquire these skills may be due to the absence of adequate training, the characteristics of various kinds of social situations, or to limitations related to neural malfunctioning. In any case, the problem is to determine what these skills are, to what extent a given individual has learned them, and for what reasons he has failed to use them in specific situations. The old concept of an inherited capacity of a broad generalized nature was useful in its day but now needs to be supplanted by many more terms describing specific problem-solving skills and the conditions, including prenatal ones, that lead to the acquisition of these skills, interfere with their acquisition, or interfere with their performance. Hopefully such an approach to individual ability will pave the way for *maximizing* everyone's potential performance rather than merely *labeling* or *classifying* their presumed inherited capacity.

Some Intelligence Tests

THE NEW REVISED STANFORD-BINET

The test now commonly known as the Stanford-Binet is the most recent of a series of revisions of the original Binet-Simon test. The first American version was made by Henry Goddard. The widely used revisions developed at Stanford University were begun by Lewis Terman in 1916 and later revised by Terman and Maud Merrill in 1937 and in 1960. The test is a mental age scale; that is, the items are organized by year levels, arranged from two years to superior adults. Although it is sometimes used for adults, the test is considered primarily a children's test and is standardized primarily with children. The Standford-Binet is generally known as a verbal scale of intelligence since it principally requires language skills for successful performance. This is not true, however, of the preschool levels; in addition, nonverbal items such as memory for drawings are scattered throughout the scale. At the younger ages typical items involve placing blocks in a form board,* naming parts of the body, naming objects shown in pictures or in miniature, identifying objects by use, repeating digits, stringing beads, giving opposite analogies, and copying geometric figures such as a diamond. Middle-age range tests include memory for digits, sentences, designs, and stories; word definition; comprehension of proper conduct; recognition of absurdities and similarities and differences; and number ability. Older-age range items emphasize vocabulary, definition of abstract words, problem-solving and reasoning, and memory for long sequences of digits and sentences.

All in all, the test is very heavily weighted with language factors, so children with foreign language backgrounds, speech handicaps, or insufficient verbal stimulation are somewhat at a disadvantage. Still, as a predictor of school performance, which itself is a highly verbal affair, the heavy emphasis on language items is very appropriate.

THE WECHSLER ADULT INTELLIGENCE SCALE (WAIS)

The WAIS, developed by David Wechsler, is another extremely widely used test of intelligence. The Wechsler scale differs from the Binet in that items similar in content are grouped into subtests and arranged in increasing order of difficulty. The Wechsler scale is generally known as a *point scale.* An individual's answers on a subtest are compared with those of a standard group of people the same age, providing a score for that subtest. The totals of the scores on the subtests are also compared with age norms. A score comparable to the Binet IQ is obtained by arbitarily setting an IQ of 100 as the score given to the average performance for any age group. Better-than-average performance would result in scores above 100, poorer-than-average performance, in scores below 100.

In order to define the average achievement or norm, Wechsler obtained test scores from a large sample of men and women of different ages. In all, his normative sample for the adult tests included 1700 subjects. These subjects were equally divided among men and women, distributed among different age groups, and selected to represent the whole country (this was accomplished by taking proportionate numbers, derived from census figures, from different parts of the country and different occupational groups).

The Wechsler scale divides verbal and performance tests into separate subsections of the instrument. In this way a verbal IQ, a performance IQ, and an over-all IQ are obtained. Even though the performance items still require a knowledge of language to understand instructions fully and to conceptualize the problems, less dependence on spoken language is necessary for correct responses than in the Stanford-Binet. The verbal tests in the scale are vocabulary, information, comprehension, arithmetic, similarities, and memory for digits. The nonverbal tests include substitution tests, picture completion, block design, arrangement of pictures, and object assembly. Wechsler also devised an intelligence scale for children (WISC) which is also now in wide use and is arranged similarly to the adult tests. The subtests are essentially similar to the adult scale. A new scale by Wechsler (Preschool and Primary Scale of Intelligence) for use with 4–6½ year–olds has recently been published; it is similar in construction to the WAIS.

PERFORMANCE SCALES

As indicated above, since the Binet and many of the other intelligence scales place a heavy emphasis on the understanding and communication of language, many psychologists felt that they tend to favor children with greater verbal stimulation at home and are unfair to those who speak a foreign language at home or who have speech or hearing handicaps. Cultural differences would probably affect language skills to a greater extent than performance skills. For example, a five-year-old from a backwoods area who had never seen an envelope could hardly be expected to define the word.

Many tests have been devised to test intellectual ability with minimum dependence on language. Form boards, the use of designs to make analogies, objects cut up into pieces, maze tracing, eye–hand coordination as in drawing and copying, recognition of errors in pictures and of missing parts —these are a few examples of performance tests. In a typical test, a wooden hand is cut up diagonally into several pieces, the pieces are presented to the subject in disarray, and his score is the time necessary to place the pieces in their correct positions. Not only are form and size perception important in obtaining a good score, but also the speed at which a subject can discover the original object from the disarrayed sections. Since speed is important, as in many intelligence test items, motivation is also an important factor.

By combining a number of such tests into a scale, a more general or stable estimate of the child's performance ability can be made than from a single test. Three such combined scales in general use are the Pintner-Patterson Scale, the Arthur Scale, and the Cornell-Cox Performance Ability Scale.

INFANT INTELLIGENCE SCALES

Although the Stanford-Binet Scale has test items starting as low as the two-year level, some psychologists have felt a need for testing even younger children. The purpose of such tests is, of course, to discover possible neuro-logical or sensory disorders that might limit development. Obviously such instruments could not depend on language. Many of the items require very simple performances—for example, following a bright object with the eyes, reaching for a box, picking up a small object, and clapping hands in imita-tion.

One test in current use is derived from the scales for normal development devised by Arnold Gesell and his co-workers. Comparison of a child's behavior with these scales yields what Gesell has called a Maturity Age Score, which, when divided by the chronological age, gives the developmen-tal quotient (DQ). Other infant scales in use are the Cattell Infant Intelli-gence Scale and the Merrill-Palmer test. Items in these tests typically measure a child's ability to maintain attention, simple eye–hand coordina-tion, the development of sensory discrimination, and the ability to point to parts of his own body.

Research has indicated that scores obtained on these tests have ex-tremely little value for predicting ability levels after age six, since many of the functions measured have only very low correlations with the later development of language skills, and since environmental stimulation has still to play a large part in the development of the child's ability. The major value of these tests lies in revealing gross disturbances in motor or sensory development. Of course, such information is of considerable value for pur-poses of examining children for potential adoption, for institutionalization, and for early treatment of some disorders.

Verbal and Performance Ability

Frequently an individual will perform significantly better on a performance scale than he will on a verbal scale, and vice versa. In a test like the WAIS, which has both verbal and performance subscales, a person then may per-form better on one half than the other. Interpretation of such differences has sometimes been rather confused. If someone does well on a perfor-mance test and there is evidence that he has been handicapped in language development, then, if he is not too old, increased verbal stimulation might lead to increased verbal ability. The opposite is true for the person who is high on verbal skills but low on performance. Many city children, for instance, have relatively little opportunity to explore some kinds of me-chanical skills, although they may be favored in items reflecting skills that can be developed by familiarity with some common widely used toys that are easily available to city children. If one accepts the notion of a basic general intelligence, then a high score in either basic kind of skill might suggest that the individual could potentially operate equally well in the other skill and is being temporally handicapped in it. In fact, however, such a score merely shows that at the present time the individual is more competent in one or the other skill.

In short, any test shows how an individual performs on a given kind of scale at a specific time. Neither verbal nor performance tests can be regarded as measuring a "true" IQ. They are different kinds of indications of ability, indications from which specific predictions can be made, as sound research has demonstrated.

Mental Deficiency

Since one of the important social tasks that psychologists in the past were called upon to perform was the measurement of intellectual ability, their skills early became crucial in the diagnosis of mental deficiency, or feeblemindedness. Even today, we have no generally accepted definition or description of mental deficiency. Some approaches stress inheritance, that is, constitutional or neurological factors; others stress social competence. In general, however, most workers in this area agree on four or five characteristics that are incorporated into most legal definitions of mental deficiency. These are listed below:

1. Mental deficiency involves the individual's inability to cope with his own society. The deficient individual presumably is not able to care for himself adequately. Such a consideration implies that mental deficiency or mental retardation is relative to the social environment. An individual at a given level of ability might be able to survive reasonably well in a simple, isolated "rural" community, but be unable to care for himself in a complex urban society where even in order to get to work and return to his home he must master an intricate transportation system.

2. The inability to care for oneself is due to an inability to learn; that is, failure is intellectual rather than emotional or motivational.

3. The low level of functioning must appear as a developmental failure. That is, the individual never matures intellectually beyond a particular level. The low level of functioning is not a result of a loss of previously learned skills, as in the case of someone who has brain damage as the result of an accident.

4. The lack of ability is considered to be stable or relatively permanent.

A definition that is widely accepted by most psychologists and is recommended for legal use by its authors, S. D. Porteus and G. R. Corbett, is, "Feebleminded persons are those who by reason of permanently retarded or arrested mental development, existing from an early age, are incapable of independent self-management and self-support."[2]

You might ask why these particular and peculiar requirements are put together to define what is presumably some mental pathology. Why does

it have to be developmental? Why is it restricted to intellectual insuffi-
ciency? The justification for this apparently peculiar definition, which obviously could not describe a single disease or disorder but, rather, only the
effects of a great many different kinds of early conditions, is that it has
certain legal or practical consequences. Once people discovered that many
children were unable to benefit from regular schools, not for reasons of
"laziness" but because of a general inability to learn, society tried to set up
some way of training such individuals or at least of protecting them when
necessary from their own inability to survive. Although the early institutions for the feebleminded, and many of the current ones, have been grossly
undersupported financially and have been able to do for the children and
adults in them only a small part of what they could do with adequate
facilities and personnel, they were set up as an attempt at social management for a group of children who needed special care. At the same time
those children who were unable to cope with school or life for other reasons
were considered to be treatable in other ways, medical or psychological.
The term mental deficiency, or feeblemindedness, therefore, is not a description of some specific disease or disorder, but rather a convenient category for a large group of individuals who have in common an assumed
inability to learn and a need for social management.

S. B. Sarason and J. Doris make a distinction between mental retardation
and mental deficiency. The mentally deficient are presumed to have brain
damage. Mentally retarded individuals have no known pathology of this
kind. They make up the largest number of individuals considered to be
"high grade" or "borderline" deficients. They are sometimes referred to as
"familial," "garden variety," "secondary," or "subcultural" mentally deficient because of the absence of observable organic pathology. It seems
likely that most of these people have limited ability partly or wholly as a
result of deprived cultural surroundings, lack of intellectual simulation,
psychological factors that interfered with learning at early ages, or any
combination of these. Although some would argue that genetic factors do,
in fact, partially affect the development of ability in such cases where there
is no known pathology, it is difficult for them to indicate what the nature
of these genetic limitations are. Evidence for such assertions comes from
studies of twins and siblings reared apart or from comparing intelligence
scores of identical twins with fraternal twins, but there is debate about the
meaning of these studies.

It is quite possible that in several cases of mental retardation there are
specific neurological malfunctions which have not been recognized but in
many cases postnatal influences must be playing a heavy role in the underdeveloped abilities since it is frequently extremely difficult to establish that
the limitations of most such individuals really existed from birth. Although

[2] "Statutory Definitions of Feebleminded in the U.S.A.," *Journal of Psychology* 35 (1953):
81–105.

it is generally believed that once these people have reached physical maturity they can benefit only in a limited way from education and stimulation, we still cannot definitely say that they would be unable to function at a higher level under optimal conditions of training and in healthy psychological environments.

WHAT ARE THE "CAUSES" OF MENTAL DEFICIENCY?

It was once believed that most mental deficiency was the result of the inheritance of a mental condition due to defective genes. Deficient people had deficient children. It is now clear, though, that the effects of inheritance are far more complex. Many conditions affect the developing fetus while in its mother's womb. A large number of children who fail to develop appear to have suffered some setback during the intrauterine period. Illnesses of the mother, excessive X-rays, and certain deficiencies in the blood (which may be inherited), rather than a gene for intelligence, may affect the development of the fetus. In addition, birth injuries, illnesses of the infant, dietary deficiencies either of pregnant mother or the developing infant, incompatibility with the mother's blood supply, and many other physical conditions may affect the development of intellectual ability through damage to the brain. Further, many children simply do not develop intellectual ability because of a lack of stimulation, a lack of experience, or an absence of response to their attempts to talk at crucial periods in their early development. Many of these understimulated children considered feebleminded, and in the past believed to be cases of "familial" feeblemindedness, were simply not able to score adequately on intelligence tests because they mirrored the culture of their own families. The children, in effect, were no brighter than the parents because the parents hadn't taught them any more than they themselves knew. By the time the youngsters reached school, sometimes having been kept out a year or two more than other children, they were already so far behind they were never able to catch up. For evidence that these children were not feebleminded through "inheritance," there are many studies of the children of feebleminded mothers who were placed in foster homes or adopted very early in life. These children attained intellectual levels approximately the same as their foster parents rather than their true parents.

One such study was conducted by Marie Skodak.[3] Skodak examined 16 children whose mothers had been judged mentally deficient, with IQs between 50 and 74. Most, if not all, of these women would be considered mentally retarded in the sense of the distinction made earlier. The fathers were of low occupational and socioeconomic status. The 16 children were placed in normal foster homes *before the age of six months.*

[3] "Children in Foster Homes; A Study of Mental Development," *University of Iowa Studies in Child Welfare* No. 16 (1939).

When they were tested at two and one-half years of age, they were found to have an average IQ of 116. At approximately five years of age their average IQ was 108. It is quite likely that these children would have had intelligence scores much closer to those of their true parents had they been kept in the restricted intellectual environment that these parents would have provided.

SOME SPECIAL KINDS OF MENTAL DEFICIENCY

The role of direct hereditary influences on mental retardation is still a matter of controversy. However, in some instances, which account for only a small percentage of the mentally retarded, specific disorders at least partially influenced by hereditary factors have been identified as causal agents. One of these is Down's syndrome, or mongolism. The name mongolism refers to the characteristically almond-shaped eyes that occur in such children. It appears to be related to a failure of chromosomal division whereby mongoloid children have forty-seven chromosomes rather than the normal forty-six. The over-all incidence of such children is very small, but the cases that do appear tend to occur more frequently when the mother is of advanced age or is having her first child late in life.

The children usually have, besides the epicanthic eye fold (which gives the appearance of slanted eyes), a fissured tongue, dry chapped skin, and certain other physical characteristics. The range of IQ of such children is wide but most scores are quite low.

Another specific condition is phenylketonuria (PKU). This is a metabolic disorder that appears to occur as a recessive genetic trait. The incidence of this disorder is extremely low in the general population, and some reduction in the severity of retardation can be effected by early dietary treatment.

A larger class of disorders associated with underdeveloped mental ability stems from brain injuries occurring at birth. Although children so afflicted make up a diverse group, they can sometimes be identified by the presence of other disorders, either sensory or motor. The presence of impaired motor coordination, paralyses, speech defects, or sensory disorders, along with intellectual deficit, is suggestive of brain injury, possibly received at birth.

In addition to the many prenatal conditions affecting the development of the central nervous system, a number of postnatal infectious diseases, developing early in childhood, may also retard the normal development of the brain. Diseases that *sometimes* have such detrimental effects include meningitis, encephalitis, and polioencephalitis. Occasionally other diseases occurring in infancy, such as mumps, diphtheria, scarlet fever, and pneumonia, may have similar effects on the development of the central nervous system.

There are many other specific, although rare, neurological conditions associated with mental retardation. Increasingly, researchers are identifying specific conditions related to the failure of development of the fetus. For example, a relationship has been established between the occurrence of mental deficiency and an incompatability of mother's and child's blood type, in this case, RH-negative mothers and RH-positive children.

As more and more of these special conditions are discovered, less and less reliance is placed on the theory of simple inheritance of low-level mentality. Rather, specific neural and hormone disorders, cultural depriva-tion, and emotional or personality problems appear to account for an in-creasing number of mental deficiencies.

THE DIAGNOSIS OF MENTAL DEFICIENCY

Although clinical psychologists can recognize certain signs of known physical disorders, the identification of physical conditions associated with lack of intellectual ability is primarily a medical and neurological problem. The *assessment* of the intellectual deficiency, however, *is* a psychological problem, and not always a simple one. The clinical psychologist must not only be able to certify that the inadequate intellectual functioning of the individual is below a specified level but that this low functioning is not the result of some temporary condition, lack of motivation in taking the test, or some specific disability that could be remedied. A child may fail to respond to many items on an intelligence test because he is socially with-drawn rather than because he is incapable. He may give wrong answers out of hostility rather than inadequacy. Hearing difficulties, rather than inability to learn, may account for his misunderstanding of instructions. All these and many other conditions must be carefully considered before a diagnosis of mental deficiency can be made, and it is increasingly evident that many misdiagnoses have been made in the past. Misdiagnoses can occur when emotional problems, problems of social adjustment, or problems related to unrecognized special defects in hearing, vision, or talking interfere with normal learning. In addition to these considerations, the psychologist must also consider a crucial aspect of the determination of mental deficiency—whether the individual can care for himself in his *own* social environment. Here, as in other applications of clinical psychology, experience, knowledge of the patient's culture, and skill are required rather than the routine ap-plication of practical techniques.

MANAGEMENT AND TRAINING

It is advisable for many of the lower-level feebleminded to be institution-alized because of the difficulty of physical care and the emotional stress that their long-term presence at home will impose on other members of the family; still, institutionalization as a permanent solution for all fee-bleminded people is certainly not necessary.

It is probably true that in many cases there has been underemphasis on what a particular feebleminded person could learn with optimal training and overemphasis on what he cannot learn because of his condition. R. Cromwell and his associates have shown in numerous studies that because of the feebleminded individual's inability to learn what others expect of him, he tends to become discouraged and so learns less than he can.[4] Studies of prolonged institutionalization indicate that the absence of intellectual stimulation, with no real attempt at training, results in a continuous loss of ability.

As for those classified as moron or borderline, there is no question that they can be taught to carry out socially useful activities. The problems here lie primarily in providing adequate supervision and in providing the emotional security and stability necessary to get along in spite of limited intellectual resources. The case described below illustrates this point very clearly.

HELEN: A CASE STUDY

The problem. Helen was an eighteen-year-old girl brought to the clinic by her parents, who complained of her violent outbursts of temper and her refusal to leave her room for long periods of time. She had been previously diagnosed as mentally retarded and had been removed from school when she was fourteen years old.

Helen's background. Helen was the first child born to a couple who had married relatively late in life. Her father had a small insurance business. Her mother was formerly a secretary but did not work after marriage. A brother three years younger was apparently normal and making satisfactory progress in school.

Helen was described by her parents as being slow in development. At the time she was seen by the psychologist she was about five feet tall and somewhat overweight; her legs, arms, and fingers tended to be short and stubby. When it became apparent that Helen was not walking and talking at the same age as other children, the family physician felt that she might have a thyroid deficiency of a mild type and some thyroid treatment was begun. However, this was not until Helen was already past four years of age.

Her parents were quite solicitous about her and tended to be somewhat overprotective, so she did not start school until a year later than other children. Her parents reported that she was a relatively placid baby and was good-natured both at home and at school. She was kept in the first grade for two years. That she was smaller than the other children and had diffi-

---

[4] "A Social Learning Approach to Mental Retardation." In N. L. Ellis, ed. _Handbook of Mental Deficiency_ (New York: McGraw-Hill Book Company, 1963).

culty with the work seemed to provide adequate reasons for holding her back. Later on she was failed in two other grades, and by her last year in school she was becoming a "problem." She did not want to attend school, where she was described as sullen and inattentive. Helen did learn to read in school, though her retention was poor, and she could do simple arithmetic involving adding and subtracting, but was otherwise poor in work with numbers.

Although Helen originally had had some friends, as she progressed in school she tended to be isolated rather than rejected by the other children. Her parents attempted to keep her busy or entertained at home when she was not at school. No special classes for the mentally retarded were available in her school system.

After she left school at the age of fourteen, Helen spent almost all her time at home helping her mother and was generally, according to her mother, a real help in housework, cooking, and cleaning. At the age of sixteen she worked for a short time in a nearby restaurant washing dishes, but the parents made her give up this job because they thought the work was physically taxing, and because in general they felt some shame about having a mentally retarded daughter out in the community. It was following her return to her home after this job that she began to have temper tantrums when frustrated. She did make occasional trips downtown by bus to buy simple things for herself, but her mother never trusted her with the family shopping. She also went, generally by herself but sometimes with her father, to high school football and basketball games and to movies. When refused permission to do something that she wanted to do, she would become angry, sometimes have a tantrum, and on one or two occasions struck her mother.

Intelligence testing showed a fairly even performance for both verbal and performance tasks. Her over-all intelligence quotient was around 75, which would place her on an intelligence level at somewhat above borderline mental deficiency. An earlier test given at school had resulted in an IQ of 66 and the diagnosis of borderline mental deficiency.

Evaluation.   It was clear after talking at some length to Helen and to her parents that the absence of adequate facilities for training, the parents' oversolicitude, and their concurrent feeling of shame at having had a mentally retarded daughter had resulted in the failure to develop many of Helen's potentialities for social satisfactions and for constructive accomplishment. Helen herself seemed to have more acceptance of her limited abilities than did her parents and reportedly enjoyed her experience as a dishwasher. It was only after she found herself shut off from all types of satisfactions that she became aggressive and also began to withdraw. Although her parents were willing to give her affection and care, they apparently were unable to give her any feeling of self-acceptance or to help her find a place in the community. That her continuous frustration finally gave way to aggression and withdrawal was neither surprising nor abnormal.

It is apparent that Helen could have been leading a happier and more constructive life and that her parents could also have been leading a happier life if they and society had been more accepting of her and if she in turn could then have been more accepting of herself. As it becomes clearer and clearer to the layman that mental deficiency is the result of specific neurological disorders or a lack of healthy, stimulating environment rather than an inherited taint, such acceptance is more likely. It is possible, in many cases, to increase such acceptance, at least in relatives, through the brief use of psychotherapy with the relatives. Direct psychotherapy with higher-level mentally retarded individuals can often result in greater self-acceptance. Such treatment consists largely of giving them the acceptance, the reassurance, and the support they need so that they can accept themselves and do what they are capable of without fear of social rejection and criticism.

Numerous students of mental retardation have collected information on the jobs that retarded individuals of various mental ages are capable of performing. They include a large number of unskilled and even semiskilled occupations. For example, an adult mentally retarded individual with a mental age of eight years is able to be a painter's helper, be a stock clerk, be a rug weaver, do domestic work, operate many factory machines, and work as a presser in a cleaning establishment. Mentally deficient adults with a mental age of nine years are able to do shoe repairing, operate some printing presses, work as a farm helper (including the operation of farm machinery), operate a motion picture machine, work as a short-order cook, make pottery, and do assembling work in a factory. With a mental age of ten, a mentally retarded individual can be an electrician's helper or plumber's helper, do painting and wood finishing, be a shipping clerk, operate a sweatermaking machine, and be a salesgirl in a five-and-dime.

It is clear that there are many useful jobs in our society for people of limited ability. It may even be that many of these positions are better filled by such individuals, who might be more satisfied with relatively routine work than the persons of higher ability. In many cases difficulties of occupational placement are due more to a matter of personality adjustment and adequate training than they are to the absence of positions that high-grade mentally deficient persons could perform adequately.

As more and more of the causes of mental deficiency are discovered, it becomes increasingly possible to prevent many cases from arising and to treat others early so as to minimize the effects of the disorder. For example, early recognition of hypothyroidism followed by treatment with thyroid extract can prevent the development of cretinism. In many other cases clinical psychologists can function not only in the diagnosis of the mentally deficient but also in discovering the optimal conditions under which they can learn and what they can learn; in addition, of course, clinicians can provide the psychological treatment of the mentally deficient so that many of them can lead happier and more constructive lives.

The Measurement of Loss in Intellectual Functioning

As clinical psychologists became more interested in adult psychopathological cases and were drawn into the problems of the diagnosis of such persons, they began to look at their intelligence tests to see what they could find in addition to what they presumed to be measures of inherited ability.

In the 1920s and 1930s it was widely believed that one of the characteristics of psychosis, or insanity, was a deterioration, or loss, of intellectual ability. The longer and more seriously psychotic a person was, the more deterioration he suffered. In making a diagnosis of the degree and duration of mental disorder, it was important, therefore, to be able to determine if a patient was functioning below his previous level of ability.

The observations of many psychologists in different settings did show some general differences in the kinds of test responses of people who had functioned more efficiently or at a higher intellectual level before psychosis and those who had not. One of these differences was that people who had *lost* some ability were generally able to do better on tests involving previously well-established knowledge, such as vocabulary or certain kinds of information. They did less well, however, on tests involving a high degree of concentration and cooperation at the moment—that is, in solving difficult problems, learning new things, or remembering some immediate stimulus such as a series of numbers or sentences. They also did less well on performance tests in general, particularly when these were scored for speed. Special tests for the measurement of such dysfunction were developed early by Frederick Wells, who devised a memory scale, which was later revised by David Wechsler. Later, Walter Shipley developed a test that contrasted the individual's performance on a multiple-choice vocabulary test with his performance on a series of increasingly difficult analogical reasoning problems.

Although it could readily be shown that most of these generalizations held up for large samples, there were, of course, many individual discrepancies. Attempts were made also to compare the subtests or subscales of such instruments as the Wechsler Intelligence Scale described earlier, and to break down the Stanford-Binet into types of subtests, in the hope of finding a pattern, or profile, of subtests characteristic of different kinds of disorders. Some psychologists felt that very specific patterns of subtests could identify particular mental disorders, but in general, research has not supported these views. What seems to be more typical is that in any kind of pathology, temporary or permanent, that leads to poorer mental functioning, those tests that require attention, cooperation, effort, motivation, and concentration have a higher probability of showing impairment than those that reflect older, more established learnings.

Psychologists have also been depended upon to help determine the presence or absence of damage to the brain. It is only relatively recently that neurologists and physicians have developed more accurate physiological techniques of identifying damage to the association areas* of the brain. Thus, in many cases it used to be extremely difficult to determine whether a patient was suffering from what was called "a functional" disorder, meaning one where there was no known physical or physiological pathology, or from true damage to the nervous system. Frequently, to make such a differential diagnosis, it was necessary to wait such a long time that it was difficult to institute measures to help the patient. To deal with this problem, psychologists were called on to use their tests to differentiate patients whose low functioning was a result of damage or insult to the brain from those who had always performed at their present level. In general, psychologists have been able to work fairly successfully at making this differentiation when the patient's behavior did not resemble the behavior of a "mentally" disturbed patient. But they have found it far more difficult to separate those patients whose loss of ability was a result of "functional" conditions (psychosis or insanity) from those whose bizarre or unusual behavior, apathy, or inability or refusal to talk was a result of damage to the brain.

One example of research on test patterns is an investigation by Ann Magaret, who compared the Wechsler-Bellevue Adult Intelligence Scale subtest scores of 80 patients diagnosed as schizophrenic (a functional psychosis) with 40 patients diagnosed as psychotic with general paresis (a psychosis associated with damage to the brain). Both groups' subtest patterns were compared to 210 normal subjects of the same age range, taken from Wechsler's normative sample.

Table 2 shows the average score for each group on each of the subtests and the rank of each subtest from highest (1) to lowest (11) to show differences in the *pattern* of abilities. It is likely that the patient sample was somewhat lower in intellectual ability before the onset of the disorder.

It can be seen that there are gross differences on the over-all level of scores for the three groups. Although the patient group prior to the onset of disorder was somewhat lower in ability, it is evident that illness has resulted in a serious decrement in intellectual functioning, with the brain-damaged (paretic) patients suffering the most. It can also be seen that the range of differences in the subtest averages was greater for the patient groups than the normal subjects. A look at the pattern of subtest averages as shown by the ranks of the subtests shows that the patient samples are quite similar to each other. The best two and worst two subtests for both groups are the same, even though one group is suffering from a disorder

Table 2

Average Scores and Ranks of Wechsler-Bellevue Adult Intelligence Scale Subtests for Two Patient Groups and a Normative Comparison

SUBTESTS	SCHIZOPHRENICS $N=80$		PARETICS $N=40$		NONPSYCHOTICS $N=210$	
	Means	*Rank*	*Means*	*Rank*	*Means*	*Rank*
Information	8.1	2	6.3	2	9.8	2
Comprehension	6.0	7	5.5	4	9.7	3
Arithmetic	5.4	9.5	4.0	11	9.2	8
Digits	6.6	6	4.6	8	8.9	11
Similarities	6.8	5	4.4	9	9.5	4
Vocabulary	8.5	1	7.2	1	9.8	1
Picture completion	5.8	8	5.6	3	9.3	6
Picture arrangement	5.4	9.5	4.8	7	9.0	10
Object assembly	7.4	3	5.1	6	9.2	8
Block designs	7.2	4	5.2	5	9.4	5
Substitution	5.2	11	4.1	10	9.2	8
Average of 11 tests	6.6		5.2		9.5	

From Ann Magaret, "Parallels in the Behavior of Schizophrenics, Paretics and Presenile Nonpsychotics," *Journal of Abnormal and Social Psychology* 37 (1942): 511–28, by permission.

without known organic damage and the other is known to have serious damage to the brain. In both cases overlearned material (information and vocabulary) is relatively good and tests requiring concentration, speed, and effort (arithmetic and substitution) are poorest.

What these and other findings indicate is that the clinical psychologist can be of considerable value in discovering the presence of pathological brain functioning and loss of intellectual ability as a result of serious nonorganic disorders. But when an organic patient's symptoms are similar to those of a functional psychotic patient, as in paresis, the psychologist must be much more cautious in reaching conclusions. In such cases, if the psychologists' tests are to be considered only indicators for more rigorous neurological studies rather than evidence of organic brain disorder, then the use of such tests can be of considerable value.

Personality Diagnosis

chapter four

Gordon Allport has reported that there are 18,000 terms in the English language that can be used to describe unique characteristics of individual behavior, or personality.[1] A large share of these terms can be used to describe abnormal, unusual, or psychopathological behavior. Clearly, if a clinical psychologist sets out to describe the relatively constant, generalized characteristics of people, there are a great many possible concepts he might use. How is he to select the most basic, most important, or most valuable? If he were to give only one test, should it measure honesty, cheerfulness, the potential to be hostile to others, the ability to deal with problems rationally, impulsiveness, optimism, sociability, or what? In fact, if he were to have the time and opportunity to try to assess, by testing and other means, fifty different characteristics, he would still face the problem of which fifty to choose from the potential hundreds of possible descriptive terms.

The answer is that any particular clinical psychologist draws his concepts from theories about personality or psychopathology. Sometimes these theories are carefully described and explicit, the assumptions in the theories

[1] *Personality: A Psychological Interpretation* (New York: Holt, Rinehart, & Winston, Inc., 1937).

45

being made known and all the terms carefully defined. In other instances the theories accumulate over a period of time, the assumptions are never made clear, and definitions of terms are vague. Nevertheless, these theories too may have definite implications for what is central to the study of personality or psychopathology. One theory of the latter type, which has rarely been made explicit yet at one time dominated the thinking of people working in the field of abnormal behavior, is the disease-entity approach to psychopathology.

Before going on to discuss the methods that psychologists use in measuring or diagnosing personality, it will be useful to discuss four broad groupings of theories of personality that contribute a large share of the concepts typically used by clinical psychologists.[2]

The Disease-Entity Approach

In the Middle Ages, people whose behavior was bizarre, peculiar, irrational, or incomprehensible were considered to be possessed by devils or spirits. To rid them of such demons, they were sometimes tortured and occasionally they were burned as witches. Gradually a more humane approach to socially deviant behavior arose and a decided effort was made by the educated to understand, rather than persecute, such aberrations. The physicians of the nineteenth century managed slowly to convey the notion that these were illnesses and that the people subject to them should be regarded as sick rather than damned. When the process of describing the essential nature of these illnesses began, the medical approach was naturally brought to bear on psychological disorders. As with other kinds of diseases, it was first assumed that each individual was suffering from some specific disorder, which was revealed by symptoms of observable behavior, and that clusters of these symptoms would identify the underlying basic disease. The prevailing view, then, was that mental illnesses are like those physical illnesses wherin a characteristic pattern of symptoms fits most afflicted individuals, as in gout, a malfunction of the gall bladder, a tumor of the brain, an eruption of an inflamed appendix, or an attack upon the lungs by the tuberculosis bacilli. As the descriptions of "diseases" accumulated, attempts at over-all classification began to appear, culminating in the work of Emil Kraepelin in the latter part of the nineteenth century. Kraepelin, a German physician who also trained in psychology, made a rather thorough and systematic classification of the mental disorders then described primarily in the French and German literature.

---

[2] For a somewhat different discussion of some of these approaches and other points of view that is not so specifically oriented to problems of clinical psychology, see the volume by Richard S. Lazarus, *Personality,* in this series.

Kraepelin's first major classificatory breakdown was into organic (endogenous) disorders and functional (exogenous) disorders. In the organic disorders, he assumed that the psychopathology was associated with some known physical or physiological pathology. In the functional disorders no such physical or physiological pathology was known at the time. It should be clear that in both cases the existence of physical pathology in itself did not describe a psychological disorder. That disorder lay in the way the individual thought and acted, but in some instances it was felt that the affliction was caused by or related to known organic pathology. Early classifiers frequently assumed these organic pathologies on rather limited evidence; since then a number of disorders have been transferred from one major Kraepelinian category to another on the basis of new information.

Although the Kraepelinian diagnostic schema has been changed, refined, and improved upon over the years, it is still the basic classificatory schema used by psychiatrists and to a large extent by abnormal psychologists. It is sometimes referred to as the psychiatric classification system or psychiatric nosology.

The basic principles of classification for the diagnostic schema now in use are varied and relatively unsystematic. Some disorders are identified not so much from their symptoms as from their presumed causes—particularly the organic psychoses, such as psychosis resulting from drug intoxication. Other disorders are identified almost entirely by their symptoms—for example, in hysterical neurosis the patient experiences a loss of function in some sensory or muscular organ of the body. Still others are identified by prognosis—for example, it is assumed that schizophrenia is more likely to last over long periods of time than depression. In this case the duration of the illness itself is used as one of the bases for classification.

Examples of organic disorders, or disturbances in thinking and action associated with psychological abnormality, are tumors, deteriorative brain disorders, drug intoxications, attacks on the central nervous system by the syphilis spirochete (paresis), and aftereffects of damage to the brain from such diseases as encephalitis (postencephalitis). The symptoms in these disorders vary over a considerable range including delusions* and hallucinations*. In some cases symptoms may wrongly give the appearance of bizarre thinking processes, as in the aphasias, where language functions are disturbed. Here, either the individual is unable to understand or properly interpret language, or he is unable to express his own thoughts. Such disorders, usually related to some damage to the association areas of the brain, may sometimes give the appearance of "psychiatric" disorders where similar behavior is not related to any known organic pathology.

The functional disorders are divided into three major groupings. One of these is the psychoses. The term psychosis is roughly equivalent to the common use of insanity. An individual diagnosed as psychotic usually loses his civil rights and can be placed in a hospital without his own consent.

Since the term has legal implications, the diagnosis of psychosis has important practical consequences. Yet the definition of a psychosis cannot be easily formulated. In general, psychosis involves a distortion of the environment resulting from abnormal processes of thought, perception, and emotional reaction. The distortion is of sufficient degree that a patient is considered to be unable to take care of himself adequately and may represent a danger to himself or others.

Schizophrenia is the functional psychotic disorder that presumably occurs in our culture most often. It is characterized by delusions, hallucinations, extremely withdrawn behavior, and confused or irrational thinking, and an inability to respond with appropriate emotions. Severe disturbances in emotional reactivity are labeled manic–depressive psychosis. The manic aspect is evidenced by heightened excitement, the depressive by inappropriate sadness and discouragement. Severely depressed patients are frequently considered suicidal risks. A disorder characterized by ideas (delusions) of persecution so systematized that they appear almost rational, except for the basic assumptions on which they are made, is referred to as paranoia. Depressions and other serious symptoms that come late in life, the onset appearing to be roughly coincident with the involutional period,* have been described as involutional melancholia.

The second large grouping of functional disorders comprises the psychoneuroses. In this case, although the individual is unhappy, maladjusted, and sometimes peculiar in his behavior, the distortions of reality are not as gross as in psychoses, and the individual is frequently able to cope with various aspects of his environment. The paragraph quoted below will help distinguish the "neurotic" from the "psychotic."

> ...The neurotics may sometimes be just as seriously disabled [as the psychotics], but the disturbances of their psychic life are less severe and the personality does not show the signs of complete disorganization. They are usually well oriented for time, place, and person; and while their insight does not enable them to understand the reasons for their difficulties, they are able to recognize the fact that the difficulties exist. Although their indulgences in fantasy may be extreme, they are able to distinguish fact from fancy. Finally, they do not suffer the extensive disorganization of personality in which delusions and hallucinations are exhibited.[3]

In psychoneurosis the symptoms may lie in exaggerated fears, obsessive thoughts that recur with great persistence, specific ideas regarding sexual behavior that interfere with normal sexual adjustment, and the

[3] From G. W. Shaffer and R. S. Lazarus, *Fundamental Concepts in Clinical Psychology* (New York: McGraw-Hill Book Company, 1952), p. 292, by permission.

presence of physical complaints that have no apparent physiological basis (tiredness, weakness, headaches, paralysis, loss of sensation, and so on). Other symptoms may include, for example, exaggerated feelings of inadequacy, extreme shyness, anxiety, and feelings of continuous tension.

The third large grouping of functional disorders consists of the psychopathic personalities. Originally believed to be constitutional—that is, primarily hereditary in nature—these disorders are generally characterized by behavior that is amoral or in opposition to the standards of society. Although few now consider this class of disorders to be hereditary, it is still employed to describe highly stable and difficult-to-change patterns of behavior. Included here are the habitual criminals, chronic alcoholics, drug addicts, sexual deviates, and those who appear (sometimes deceptively) to lack common feeling with others in their society.

Approaching personality description or diagnosis via such a classification schema necessarily involves measuring the characteristics, or symptoms, predominant in the various disorders. So, tests must be devised to determine if an individual's thinking processes are rational, if he is suffering from hallucinations or delusions, if his emotional reactions are normal, and so forth. The outcome of such observations would facilitate diagnosis. Although psychologists and psychiatrists are now aware of the limitations of this approach, in many settings it is still quite influential in determining the activities of the clinical psychologist. We can briefly summarize some of those limitations as follows:

1. As a general approach to personality description it does not account for the individual differences in the large group of people who are "normal." Approaches to describing such people have been limited, therefore, to describing their tendencies towards psychopathological behavior, still leaving out major aspects of their personalities.

2. The clear-cut facts are that the symptom pictures do not fall into neat patterns or clusters. There is considerable overlap in the symptoms of different disorders, and many people seem to be as much mixtures of different disorders as representative of a single one. As a result, diagnosis is highly unreliable; it frequently changes with time and can differ markedly with the diagnostician.

3. Since we have increased our understanding of the experience behind many pathological behaviors, it now seems clear that different individuals may develop the same symptoms for different reasons and that, equally, individuals with similar difficulties (as understood in terms of their underlying etiology) may develop many different symptoms. In other words, the disease model carried over from medicine is simply inappropriate to the field of psychological abnormality. In abnormal psychology the evidence is very strong that we are dealing with the results of people's experience and not with the effects of disease processes.

4. The general approach of diagnosis appears to be fairly sterile. In the hundred years or so since these diagnostic entities presumably have been identified and described, it has been extremely difficult, particularly in the case of the functional

disorders, to find any appropriate methods of treatment that follow from the diagnosis. That is, classification seems to exist merely for the sake of classification, and specific treatments for the specific disorders are simply lacking.

The Faculty, Type, and Trait Approach

Although it is somewhat unfair to include the modern trait approach to personality alongside the outmoded approaches based on faculties of the mind or personality types, it is probably true that the trait approach has evolved from these earlier approaches and still has some characteristics in common with them.

FACULTY PSYCHOLOGY

A faculty might be described as an innate capacity of "mind-in-general" —that is, it is a characteristic or universal attribute of human beings. Each faculty is considered to be an independent entity that, although it can be influenced by other faculties and can influence others, maintains a separate existence. An individual might not fully develop some capacity; on the other hand, he might develop it as fully as nature (inheritance) will allow.

Faculty psychology has rarely been set forth as a carefully defined doctrine. Although few modern psychologists are adherents of faculty psychology, many are influenced by its concepts. Faculty psychologists differ in the degree to which they stress the innateness of faculties and the degree to which they hold that faculties influence one another. Individual faculty psychologists also differ in the degree to which they are concerned with general characteristics of the mind and with individual differences. Even when the immediate concern of any faculty theorist seems to be only the definition of a new faculty of the mind, the ultimate purpose is to produce a variable upon which individuals can be compared.

There are many classifications of the faculties of the mind, dating from the time of the early Greeks. Will, reason, sagacity, imitation, love, pity, and vanity are some of the many faculty concepts that have appeared in descriptions of man's character through the centuries. They are related to lists of instincts (for instance, gregariousness, imitation, sympathy, domination) that have been popular at various times.

You might well ask what, if anything, is wrong with faculty psychology, since these terms and concepts would not have persisted were they not useful. The usual criticism of the faculty approach is that it explains by classifying. The answer to the question, Why does he perceive color, manipulate tools, remember digits? is, He has color perception, mechanical ability, and memory. In the field of individual differences, the answer is that he has a greater or lesser amount of the faculty than the average. Obviously there is enough generality between remembering digits, remembering names, and remembering lessons (although it is indeed far from a perfect relationship) to warrant some predictability to a concept of memory for some practical purposes. But there is a great danger when such a descriptive construct is used in lieu of a fuller explanation or description of the conditions under which an act occurs or does not occur, since the latter information allows for prediction and control and the former does not. Honesty, for example, as a faculty does not fare so well, for it has been convincingly demonstrated that honesty in one situation can be wholly unrelated to behavior in another.

Perhaps a more general criticism of faculty psychology is that it makes entities out of *constructed aspects* of behavior. These entities are treated as if they reside within the individual, and much wasted effort goes into identifying them, classifying them, and devising tests to measure them instead of devising tests to solve such practical problems as how to train people to exercise good judgment or how to prevent and treat mental disorder. It is a static philosophy in which behavior is predicted on the basis of relatively independent entities within the person rather than on the basis of a complexly organized individual in interaction with a complexly organized environment.

TYPOLOGIES

A typology is a system of classifying individuals into very broad categories or types. Typologies, in common with the faculty approach, attempt to predict behavior without requiring a description of the environmental situation in which the behavior occurs. They explain on the basis of an internal, relatively unchanging characteristic of the individual. Even more than the faculty approach, typologies usually have at their base genetic or constitutional assumptions. A person is presumed to behave the way he does because of inherited characteristics or of constitutional characteristics that are probably largely inherited.

In the sense that typological theories do not have principles for characterizing the effects of interaction between the individual and the environment, they are static. They are static also in the sense that they tend to explain on the basis of relatively unchanging characteristics, rather than in terms of behavior that is learned and susceptible to change. A third restricting characteristic of typologies is the limited number of descriptive concepts they employ. Typologies that try to explain behavior by characterizing individuals into two, three, or four types—and even seven basic types as in A. J. Rosanoff's approach—are extremely limited in their ability to describe and predict complex behavior of human beings.

Although typologies have flourished from the time of the early Greeks, present-day typological concepts in psychology are predominantly influenced by the French school, represented by the work of Louis Rostan in

1828, and by the German school of Ernst Kretschmer, whose typology followed closely that of Rostan's, and like his was based primarily on body characteristics. Rostan categorized into a digestive type, a muscular type, a respiratory type, and a cerebral type. These types correspond rather closely to Kretschmer's pyknic, athletic, athletic-asthenic, and asthenic types (see discussion of Sheldon following). Even when a typology includes the possibility of more or less of something, so that a given individual has a place on the continuum of a single trait or has various degrees of several, we are still faced with a narrow, limited, and crude method of describing human behavior.

The present-day development of the Rostan and Kretschmer typology is best exhibited in the work of William H. Sheldon.[4] Although Sheldon has worked out one of the most elaborate typological systems with the most objective referents for classification purposes, he remains subject to the criticisms of all typologies. Sheldon distinguishes three body types. The *endomorph* (the digestive–pyknic) is characterized by massive digestive viscera and relatively weak development of somatic structures (bone, muscle, and connective tissues). Endomorphs are usually fat but they sometimes may seem emaciated. They are of low specific gravity. In the second type, the *mesomorph,* the somatic structures are in the ascendency (muscular–athletic). There is an uprightness and sturdiness of structure. Bone, muscle, and connective tissue are predominant. The skin is relatively thick, with large pores. In *ectomorphy* (asthenic–leptosomic–cerebral) the structure is fragile and linear; the chest is flat and extremities are long, slender, poorly muscled, with pipestem bones. Posture is stooped and there is a hesitant restraint of movement.

Corresponding to these three body types are three temperament types: visceratonia, the personality of the endomorph; somatotonia, the personality of the mesomorph; and cerebratonia, the personality of the ectomorph. The *visceratonic* likes to eat and to socialize, he needs affection and approval, is complacent and tolerant, and expresses emotion freely. The *somatotonic* is assertive, ambitious, and aggressive, he loves exercise, risk, and competion, and attempts to solve problems with action. The *cerebratonic* is restrained, reflective, secretive, and overly reactive. He likes solitude and is self-conscious and inhibited in social expression.

Individuals, then, do not have to be classified as pure types, but rather are classified on a seven-point scale showing degrees of tendency in all the soma and temperament types. Many difficulties remain with such an approach, however. It is assumed, for example, that individuals have all the traits attributed to all three temperamental types to the same degree as their rating on the morphological scales. Even if it can be demonstrated that some low-order correlations exist between constitution and meaningful behavior,

[4] *The Varieties of Human Physique* (New York: Harper and Brothers, 1940).

or between meaningful behaviors in groups of people classified according to constitution, such classifications have little predictive value for describing behavior in any specific situation. Furthermore, if such correlations are shown to exist, it is a matter of interpretation whether they are biologically determined or whether they depend on the cultural and personal reactions to the bodily differences that exist between individuals. A thin, frail boy may have esthetic interests and asocial hobbies not because of genetic determinations but rather because, in a given culture, he does not find satisfaction in sports and physical play and consequently is forced to seek satisfaction in asocial hobbies such as reading. That the physical typologies such as Sheldon's do not seem to be applicable to females of the same culture, whose roles in childhood and adulthood are unlike the males', suggests that the differences found depend on the uniformity of cultural reactions rather than biological determination.

Jung's typology of extrovert and introvert[5] is primarily a psychological rather than a constitutional typology, such as those discussed above. It overlaps heavily, nevertheless, with the description of the psychological characteristics of the constitutional types. In general, the introvert is similar to the asthenic, leptosome, or ectomorph individual and the extrovert is similar to the digestive, pyknic, or endomorphic individual. Subtypes and elaborations, such as an ambivert who is both extroverted and introverted or the false extrovert who is apparently outgoing actually egocentric and seeking power, would overlap with the muscular, athletic, or mesomorphic type.

TRAIT PSYCHOLOGY

The trait approach to the description of behavior has several points in common with the typological approach. Gordon Allport, however, has drawn a very interesting differentiation between typologies and the trait approach. According to Allport, "A man can be said to *have* a trait; but he cannot be said to *have* a type. Rather, he *fits* a type." In its modern usage, a trait is a variable, or a continuum upon which individuals may be placed. Allport makes a special case for idiosyncratic or individual traits that are characteristic of only one person, but it is not clear how such characteristics may be described, understood, or predicted for scientific purposes. As for more general or nomothetic* traits, the sharp difference that Allport makes seems to break down into a matter of degree rather than one of kind.

Sheldon places individuals on a continuum in his typology. It differs from some trait systems in using relatively few variables and in supposing that each variable tends to be representative of a cluster of characteristics that would be considered as traits. Trait systems are not as limited, as typologies

---

[5] *Psychological Types* (New York: Harcourt, Brace and Company, 1923).

are , by having too few categories or by making too few distinctions regarding individual differences. The major fault of a trait system, however, like that of faculty psychology, lies in dealing with personality as some internal characteristic without utilizing the situation for prediction. If an individual is at the average, or 50th percentile, for the trait of aggression, does this mean he will always act half-way aggressive, act aggressive half of the time (and if so, which half of the time), or what? This limitation is not a necessary one, however. It would be possible to describe traits in situational terms or to describe traits in terms of the directionality of behavior in a way not unlike the concept of psychological needs discussed later in this chapter.

A trait or habit approach to personality description is further limited if it does not provide conditions for change as a result of interaction with the environment. It is possible, however, to think of a trait as a habit. Integrated with learning theory, this approach can provide a terminology for describing not only behavior but also changes in behavior.

The personality theories of Gordon Allport and Raymond Cattell are representative of modern approaches to trait psychology. Allport emphasizes many traits, including unique traits or unique combinations of traits that may characterize only one or a few persons. He gives "fastidious exhibitionism" as an example of such a trait. Cattell is more interested in traits common to everyone such as gregariousness. By the use of statistical techniques (factor analyses) he hopes to reduce the number of trait names to as few independent descriptive terms as possible and still obtain useful predictions.

In general, traits differ from types and from faculties in that they are not as likely to involve assumptions about inherited or constitutional origins. They differ in that they provide potentially a much larger number of ways of describing the infinite variety of human behaviors, including a concept of interacting traits that increases the potential for prediction. Approaches that are limited solely to the description of traits, however, neglect the importance of the environment in the determination of behavior and fail particularly to develop principles to describe that interaction and to describe and predict change in personality. Such trait theories usually fail to recognize all behavior as potentially predictable and consistent; rather they accept inconsistency as being characteristic of a weak trait.

The Psychoanalytic Approach

The term psychoanalysis often generates much confusion in discussion and argument. It sometimes refers to a series of observations about human nature made by Sigmund Freud and many of his followers. Sometimes it refers to the theory of personality and method of psychological treatment promulgated by Freud (which is the way we shall use it here). Sometimes it refers to other personality theories that have something in common, but also many points of difference, with Freud's views—such theories as those of Alfred Adler, Otto Rank, and Harry S. Sullivan. Although many of the ideas put forth by Freud have now been modified or rejected by current adherents of psychoanalysis, there seems to be little doubt that his work has had more influence on current theories of personality than that of any other single person. His ideas have extended far beyond psychology into all the other social sciences, and into the educational system and child-raising practices of Western civilization.

Although it is not possible in this brief exposition to describe psychoanalytic theory in any great detail, we must consider those aspects that are of particular importance for understanding the assessment and diagnosis of personality.

One of Freud's major contributions was his theory of *psychic determinism.* In contrast to faculty and type theories, which assume that the important characteristics of human behavior are simply general in the species, Freud's position was that human behavior is motivated, or directed, toward obtaining specific goals. He stated that all human behavior, including the psychopathological, has meaning. In other words, he felt that the symptoms of an abnormal person are not merely indications of some breakdown in the organism, as are the symptoms of physical illnesses, but that they have particular significance in light of the individual's goals or motives. What the symptoms reveal is not disease but conflict in the mind. Having been trained as a physician, however, Freud felt the need to assert an energy source for goal-seeking behavior, which source he found in biologically rooted instincts. The individual, he claimed, seeks only to obtain pleasure and avoid pain; his inherited instincts determine at any particular time what is pleasurable. Freud, to the consternation of many, held that sexual instincts are the primary source of motivation for most human behavior.

Along with his notion of psychic determinism, his other great contribution was *unconscious motivation.* Although other psychologists and philosophers had recognized that man was moved sometimes by unconscious motives, none gave this idea such prominence as did Freud. He postulated an unconscious mind, not only as a repository for many of the instincts for pleasure and destruction, but also as a repository for ideas, feelings, or wishes that an individual will not accept about himself—associations, ideas, or desires he strives to forget or avoid. Freud referred to these thoughts as repressions. He conceived of the mind in terms of these forces acting upon the person and frequently warring within him for control. Because of the moral strictures of society, the taboos and punishment imposed for uninhibited gratifications of sexual and hostile urges, a person has to repress many of his desires, but the energy involved in seeking such gratification remains present and may result in severe inner conflicts.

The unconscious impulses are able to escape through symbolism,* however, in dreams, in symptoms, in fantasies, and in other ways. Sometimes these unconscious impulses are revealed by the very ways an individual defends himself against their entering his conscious mind—for instance, by overvigorous denial of some impulse or by projecting it onto others (for example, by saying, "It is not I who am angry but you"). Additional aspects of psychoanalysis will be discussed in the next chapter, concerning psychotherapy.

The effect of the psychoanalytic movement, with its emphasis on unconscious mechanisms, was to complicate enormously the problem of diagnosis. Symptoms themselves now had less meaning and one had to go behind them for the internal conflicts. One could not expect to discover the important aspects of an individual from asking direct questions. Not only might he consciously wish to cover up information, but also, the psychoanalytic approach implies, he might not be aware of his own problems. In order to discover these, far more subtle and ingenious methods had to be designed.

Many criticisms have been leveled at orthodox, or Freudian, psychoanalysis as well as at the modern versions. The major criticism deals with the reliance on instincts as a source of energy for goal-directed behavior, the complaint being that the strength of these instincts or the conditions that produce them are never described. Consequently, they are used to *explain after the fact* rather than before. The second general criticism hits at the difficulty of measuring the concepts used in psychoanalysis. In short, it is difficult to determine reliably when some process is going on and to what degree. Related to this shortcoming, or as a result of it, it has been extremely difficult objectively or experimentally to test many psychoanalytic hypotheses.

Nevertheless, the contributions of psychic determinism and unconscious motivation are widely accepted in modern theorizing about personality. Both principles lead to the recognition that the problem of understanding and predicting human behavior is an exceedingly complex one involving great skill and ingenuity and one unlikely to be solved by the construction of a few relatively simple tests or measures.

The Psychological-Need Approach

As a result of the Freudian influence, many personality theorists began to rely more and more on analysis of the motive, or direction, of behavior. Some theorists, however, rejected Freud's emphasis on sex, or the instinctual basis for the motivation, or both. There were also attempts by American psychologists (with their emphasis on measurement) to devise ways of classifying behaviors in terms of their directionality that would allow for reliable measurement while still remaining within the basic framework of psychoanalysis. The classification of Henry Murray, to be described below, is primarily of this kind.[6] Other attempts to describe basic human motivations, such as that of W. I. Thomas as early as 1923, approached the problem from a sociological point of view with an emphasis on strong goals common to the culture, such as the needs for social status, love, independence, and power.

All these classifiers characteristically list a set of terms (called needs or motives) that abstract behavior. These terms differ from traits in that a general concept is derived not so much from the objective similarity of behavioral referents as from similarity of the goals or underlying motivating forces. As with trait lists, an attempt was made to avoid overlap among concepts, but this was difficult to achieve and usually no principle was employed to maintain a uniform level of generality. Since terms were differentially inclusive of others, one might partly subsume another. The most frequent basis used by theorists of this kind for selecting concepts or terms to abstract commonality from behaviors was either intuitive experience or extrapolations from psychoanalysis of specific kinds of sexual drives.

Murray substituted needs for Freud's instincts, but he retains many of Freud's other hypotheses about behavior. He also has emphasized that the understanding of behavior must include an analysis of environmental conditions, which he called *presses.* A press is a property of the environment that helps or hinders an individual to reach some specific goal.

Some thirty needs employed by Murray are listed below. These are not the only variables in Murray's system. They do exemplify an attempt to describe behavior in terms of its direction, conceived of as needs.

Abasement	Deference	Play
Achievement	Dependence	Recognition
Acquisition	Dominance	Rejection
Affiliation	Exhibition	Retention
Aggression	Exposition	Seclusion
Autonomy	Harmavoidance	Sentience
Blamavoidance	Infavoidance	Sex
Cognizance	Inviolacy	Succorance
Construction	Nurturance	Superiority
Counteraction	Order	Understanding

Murray's organization of human behavior in terms of needs and presses attempts to avoid, at least by the absence of explicit statement, the implication of instincts. He also avoids limiting most directional behavior to primary sexual drives. However, Murray's list of needs has several limitations: *(1)* The concepts were not tested for economy, overlap, or utility. *(2)* The concepts were not strictly enough defined to allow for objective measurement. *(3)* There is no indication of the prior conditions or experiences that account for the presence, absence, or strength of the various needs. This

[6] *Explorations in Personality* (New York: Oxford University Press, 1938).

approach may, nevertheless, constitute an advance over trait psychology in seeking similarity of behavior in terms of motives, rather than similarities of behavior in which the aspect of similarity that is abstracted tends to be arbitrary rather than based on consistent principle. It also places greater emphasis on the relevance of the environment in understanding behavior, through the concept of press.

Social Learning Theory

Another approach utilizing psychological needs is that of social learning theory, developed by the writer, his colleagues, and students. This is a somewhat different view of psychological needs from that of Murray, relying heavily on learning theory to account for the development and change in psychological needs.

According to social learning theory, man's behavior is determined by his goals. Behavior is always directional. An individual responds with those behaviors that he has learned will lead to the greatest satisfaction in a given situation. Each person gradually associates certain goal objects and internal conditions with unlearned or inborn satisfactions. For example, first the mother's feeding satisfies the infant; then the presence of the mother herself becomes pleasurable; then the individual may strive to do things of which the mother approves, until finally even in the absence of the mother, he takes satisfaction in the accomplishment of tasks once associated with her approval. As differentiated from the unlearned or biologically based satisfactions of the organism, the psychological motives are the result of experience rather than instinct.

Gradually a set of differentiated motives, or needs, develops in each individual, varying from very specific to very general. The more specific the category of behaviors and goals included in the need, the more possible it is to predict the strength of one from another. The more general, broad, or inclusive the concept, the less accurate the prediction of one behavior from another.

From this point of view a need has three essential components. One of these is the set of behaviors directed toward the same goal (or to similar or related ones); an example is the set of behaviors used by a person to get others to take care of him. These behaviors are called *need potentials;* the term refers to their potential strength, that is, the likelihood that they will be used in certain given situations.

The second major component is the expectancies that certain behaviors will lead to satisfactions or goals that a person values. An individual may have learned many ways of getting others to take care of him as a child, but at the present time he may have little expectation that they will lead to satisfaction. For example, crying will bring an infant care and help, but a ten or twelve-year-old boy using the same technique may find himself being rejected by his father as "a sissy." The average level of the expectations that the behaviors one has learned to rely upon to achieve certain satisfactions will actually lead to those satisfactions is referred to as *freedom of movement.*

The third general component of needs is the value *(need value)* attached to the goals themselves—that is, the degree to which an individual prefers one set of satisfactions to another. For example, given the same opportunity to obtain two satisfactions, one individual prefers to do something others will admire him for (recognition need) and another prefers to do something that will make others like him (love and affection need).

Another major aspect of social learning theory is the weight it gives to the psychological situation of the individual both in understanding and predicting his behavior. In contrast with trait or faculty approaches, or in fact any personality approach that places all the stress on internal states, this view, because of its basic learning theory assumptions, emphasizes that an individual learns through past experiences that some satisfactions are more likely in some situations than in others. Individual differences exist not only in the strength of different needs but in the way the same situation is perceived. An individual's reactions to different situations depend on his own past experience, which therefore constitutes an important aspect of individual differences. The psychological situation, then, provides the cues for a person's expectancies that his behaviors will lead to desired outcomes.

Frequently when an individual places high value on some set of goals, such as the desire for recognition or the desire to be taken care of, he may at the same time have low expectations for achieving these goals. That is, he may have learned to anticipate punishment, failure, or rejection when he attempts to achieve these desires (for example, the child who constantly obtains poor or failing grades in school). When this occurs, the person usually learns other behaviors to avoid the punishments themselves. Sometimes he tries to obtain the satisfactions by irreal* ways, such as by daydreaming or by symbolic techniques that represent to him, but to no one else, the obtaining of the satisfaction. These avoidance and irreal behaviors are *learned* and constitute what are usually regarded as the symptoms of abnormal behavior. In this view, then, abnormal behavior is not disease or disorder or breakdown but a meaningful attempt to avoid certain punishments or to obtain certain gratifications on an irreal level.

For illustrative purposes, six very broad needs, which attempt to include most learned psychological behavior, are listed below with their definitions. Actually, these terms are so broad that they permit only limited prediction, and more specific concepts are generally more useful. For example, the need for recognition and status can be easily broken down to the more specific levels of social activities, occupational or intellectual activities, and physical or athletic skills.

1. *Recognition-Status:* The need to excel, to be considered competent, good or better than others in school, occupation, profession, athletics, social position, physical appeal, or play; that is, the need to obtain high position in a socially valued competitive scale.

2. *Dominance:* The need to control the actions of other people, including family and friends; to be in a position of power, to have others follow one's own ideas and desires.

3. *Independence:* The need to make one's own decisions, to rely on oneself, to develop the skill necessary to obtain satisfaction and reach goals without the help of others.

4. *Protection-Dependency:* The need to have another person or persons prevent frustration, provide protection and security, and help obtain other desired goals.

5. *Love and Affection:* The need for acceptance and liking by other people, to have their warm regard, interest, concern, and devotion.

6. *Physical Comfort:* The need for physical satisfactions that have become associated with security and a state of well-being, the avoidance of pain, and the desire for bodily pleasures.

To sum up, the potentiality of a given behavior or set of behaviors to occur in some specific situation is dependent on an individual's expectancy that the behavior will lead to a particular goal or satisfaction, the value that satisfaction has for him, and the relative strength of other behavior potentials in the same situation. It is assumed that often the individual is unaware of the goals (or meaning) of his behavior and of the expectancies of achieving these goals.

It can be seen that the understanding and prediction of individual behavior in complex social situations is extremely difficult, requiring intensive study and much information. One particular implication of social learning theory of special importance for the procedures of assessing personality is that the situation of testing, itself, has an effect on behavior that must be taken into account before predictions from the test to other kinds of situations can be made.

From the point of view of social learning theory, not only must the individual's behavior (need potential) be assessed in diagnosing personality, but also his expectations and the values he places on different goals. It is important to know how these expectations change from situation to situation and how the obtaining of one set of satisfactions runs into conflict with another. Finally, for purposes of psychological treatment, it is frequently important to know how the expectations and values were acquired to know how best to change them. The three cases (presented earlier) of adolescent boys who stole from their teacher, are described from a social learning orientation and will help illustrate the point of view.

One experimental application of these broad needs is furnished by an investigation of Richard Jessor, Shephard Liverant, and Seymour Opochinsky.[7] These psychologists administered a forced-choice test called the Goal Preference Inventory, developed by Liverant, to four different groups of college and high school students. Later they gave subjects the Rotter Incomplete Sentences Blank, a measure of personal adjustment. In each group they obtained scores for the subjects for their expressed need for recognition and their expressed need for love and affection. They compared adjustment scores of subjects with balanced needs (both needs near the average of the group) with those showing strong imbalance. The imbalanced groups were made up of subjects who were either very high on need for recognition at the expense of need for love and affection or very high on need for love and affection at the expense of need for recognition. These results strongly supported their hypothesis that an imbalance in these two broad, important needs was related to maladjustment in our society, regardless of which need was higher.

In social learning theory, needs are not the only important index of individual differences. They may differ in their attitudes toward different kinds of people (social attitudes) and the ways in which they respond to strong reinforcement or their anticipation of strong reinforcement (emotional behavior) and in the way that they approach a variety of similar situations from a problem-solving point of view. This latter concept is called a *generalized expectancy* in social learning theory. A similar concept relating only to intellectual tasks has been called higher level learning skills by Harry Harlow. But in social situations as well as intellectual tasks, we are also repeatedly faced with similar problems. For example, the extent to which a person believes that he can control what happens to him is referred to as a belief in internal control of reinforcement. A belief that one is controlled by luck, fate, or powerful others, is referred to as a belief in external control of reinforcement. Such generalized expectancies may have important consequences for how the individual responds to different kinds of therapy, how he responds to prolonged periods of stress, and other social behaviors.

Another such generalized expectancy is one of interpersonal trust, for there is evidence that there are generalized differences in the degree to which people believe others and feel that they can be depended upon to tell the truth. Such differences can affect their responses to school, psychotherapy, marriage, and almost every kind of social interaction. A measure of this generalized trust of others was developed by the author and has been used in a number of experimental studies of interpersonal trust. One investigation by Harvey Katz and the author sought to determine the influence of parents' attitudes on the trust of children. To do this Katz and Rotter selected 100 male and 100 female college students in residence who had taken the trust

---

[7] Richard Jessor, Shephard Liverant, and Seymour Opochinsky, "Imbalance in Need Structure and Maladjustment," *Journal of Abnormal and Social Psychology* 66 (1963): 271–75.

Table 3

Trust Scores of Parents of College Students

	N	MEAN
	Fathers' Trust Scores	
Male Hi Trust	27	79.6
Male Lo Trust	29	69.4
Female Hi Trust	28	73.8
Female Lo Trust	35	72.2
	Mothers' Trust Scores	
Male Hi Trust	30	77.6
Male Lo Trust	32	73.8
Female Hi Trust	33	76.7
Female Lo Trust	38	73.9

From Harvey A. Katz and Julian B. Rotter, "Interpersonal Trust Scores of College Students and their Parents," *Child Development* 40 (1969): 657–61, by permission.

scale a year earlier and who were higher or lower than the average student on interpersonal trust. The experimenter sent trust scales directly to the students' parents, asking them to fill out and return them before the weekend (when their children might come home). Fathers and mothers were asked to answer them independently. Sixty-seven percent complied, which is a very high percentage for such studies. The parents' scores on their tests are presented in Table 3.

The mean score column of Table 3 shows that in every case the parents of the higher trusting students were themselves higher in trust than the parents of the low-trust students, although some of the differences were small. The largest and most significant effect was that of fathers and sons, contrary to the prediction that would have been made by many psychoanalytically inclined psychologists who would have anticipated a more important role for mothers.

Fathers and mothers appear to play different roles in the development of trust of others in their children. Fathers seem to play a highly influential role vis-à-vis their sons, but seem to have little effect on their daughters. Mothers, on the other hand, appear to have a small and equal effect on both sons and daughters.

The highly important role that fathers play in influencing their sons' attitudes toward interpersonal trust is not surprising. The variable measured by this scale refers to expectancies for trust of groups of social agents with whom the individual comes into contact outside the family setting for the most part. Since the father is usually the major liaison agent between the family and external groups, and is more involved in the training of sons than daughters, we would expect that his influence on his son would be maximal.

This study suggests the importance of direct teaching and the importance of parents as models in the development of basic attitudes of children.

The Techniques of Personality Assessment

As the previous section shows, there is no single set of concepts that all clinical psychologists subscribe to. The kinds of information and the kinds of test a particular clinical psychologist uses to understand personality depend on his theoretical orientation. In any case, the problem is enormously complicated, and the discipline devoted to understanding individuals and making predictions about their behavior in future situations is only beginning to achieve scientific status. Of course, constant efforts are being made to increase the objectivity and accuracy of methods of assessment, but because of the fundamental difficulty, progress is slow.

The methods that clinical psychologists use will be described briefly under the following headings: the interview, the questionnaire, projective techniques, observational methods, and behavioral techniques. The methods will be described generally, with only a brief illustration of specific instruments.[8]

THE INTERVIEW

In case work clinicians rely on no method of obtaining information about a person as heavily as they do on the interview. Perhaps more than for any other evaluation procedure, the worth of the interview depends on the experience and skill of the clinician. Ability to establish rapport with the patient, to put him at ease, to reduce the patient's defensiveness or fear of criticism so that he will speak as frankly as possible about his problems, as well as ability to notice and evaluate all the patient's behaviors, are some of the basic skills necessary. In addition, knowing what kinds of leads should be followed, how to make indirect approaches when the patient resists direct questioning, and finally how to evaluate the information obtained are basic skills of a good clinician. It is usually during the interview that the clinician forms the hypotheses that he may later follow up with special tests. This device is used to obtain the case history of a patient, and the case history is the cement that puts together the many sources of information to form a coherent picture of a person.

The clinician uses not only the information obtained directly from the patient but also the information obtained from observations of the patient's behavior in general, his speech, his mannerisms, his dress and appearance, and his cooperativeness. The clinician is not restricted to the direct answers or statements of the patient. While the patient may be saying one thing, his facial expressions, bodily movements, and tone of voice may indicate to the

---

[8] Many readers of this book will be asked at some time to take personality tests for experimental or other purposes. For this reason the tests will be described in minimum detail so that the reader can still serve as an unbiased subject.

clinician that very possibly just the opposite is true. Although the patient may deny that he is ever hostile to other members of his family, careful leads by the interviewer and careful observation of all the patient's behavior while talking about the other members of the family may reveal that he is, in fact, angry at one or more of his relatives.

The techniques of interviewing can be broken down into three broad methods. The first of these is *free* interviewing. In this technique, the interviewer says as little as possible, simply asking open or leading questions, such as, "Could you tell me something about your family?" or "Could you tell me why you have come to the clinic?" Once the patient has started talking, the clinician keeps him going by nodding, saying, "um hum," and occasionally saying, "Could you tell me more about that?" This technique usually is less threatening or disturbing to the patient than direct and specific questions and allows the interviewer to see readily what is important to the patient. If the method is used exclusively, however, it may be a long time before certain kinds of important information are brought up directly by the patient.

In the *directed* interview, the second type, the interviewer knows that he wishes to cover certain kinds of information and will ask many more direct questions. Instead of the general leading question, "Could you tell me something about your childhood?" he might ask a patient specifically for history of childhood diseases, who the other children in the family were, who the father's favorite was, what his mother's personality was like, or what his father's personality was like. Although this method introduces more information than the free type and allows coverage of a number of important areas, it may be more disturbing to the patient, and it may put him more on his guard. It may also make a patient feel that his role is only to answer the questions asked and, consequently, to neglect talking about some painful subject that he feels is important but the interviewer neglects to touch on in his more direct questions.

The third method of interviewing is referred to as the *structured* interview. Here the interviewer sets up a standard condition for all interviewees. He is required to ask the same questions, generally in the same order, and to use a standard procedure for follow-up questions. Generally a psychologist uses a structured interview when he desires to obtain a rating or a numerical score for assessing some specific characteristic. Although occasionally the structured interview is employed in clinical work with patients, it is primarily used for research purposes.

Of course, all three techniques can be combined in a single interview with a patient. The interviewer, beginning more or less with the free technique, rounds out his information with more direct questions and possibly includes a brief structured interview to measure some particular variable at the end of his clinical interview. Although it is difficult to conceive of obtaining a well-rounded picture of an individual, including the relation of his past experience to his present behavior, without an interview, the major problem involved in this technique lies in the lack of an objective way of evaluating the information obtained. The interview furnishes the clinician with many hypotheses, but some of these may reflect his own biases* or may be based on hunches without sufficient information. Consequently, judgments made from interviews must be treated with caution. Most psychologists prefer to supplement subjectively interpreted interviews with more objective tests.

THE QUESTIONNAIRE

The questionnaire played a prominent role in the early attempts to measure personality in the United States. Generally, a subject is confronted with a series of statements and asked to indicate whether the statements are true or false about himself, or whether he cannot decide or does not know. Sometimes he is asked whether or to what degree he agrees or disagrees with the statement. Such agreement is generally indicated by checking a scale such as that shown below. In other types of questionnaires the subject has to state which of two alternatives is more true of him. This is called the forced-choice method, and the choices are generally arranged so that the statements are equally positive or negative. Consequently, the subject cannot avoid making some negative statements about himself. These various types are illustrated below and are easily recognizable. They have been made up for purposes of illustration and are not taken from any specific test.

TRUE-FALSE TYPE

Circle *true* if the statement below is true about you, circle *false* if it is untrue and circle the question mark if you do not know or cannot make up your mind.
? True False 1. I frequently get headaches when something upsets me.
? True False 2. I generally am heavily influenced by others' opinions before making up my mind about important decisions.

AGREEMENT SCALE

Make a check on the scale after each statement to indicate the *degree* to which the statement is true of you.
1. I get headaches when something upsets me.

| never | rarely | sometimes | often | always |

2. I am heavily influenced by others' opinions when I have to make important decisions.

| never | rarely | sometimes | often | always |

FORCED-CHOICE TYPE

Please place a check next to *one* statement in each pair which you consider to be *more* true about you. One statement *must* be checked in each pair.
1. a. I am more likely to get headaches when something upsets me.
   b. I am more likely to become very irritable when something upsets me.
2. a. When making an important decision I often rely on the advice of others.
   b. I often act impulsively when I have to make important decisions.

For clinical purposes one of the more widely used tests with adolescents and adults is the Minnesota Multiphasic Personality Inventory (MMPI). This test contains a great many true-false items (550) and requires from 45 minutes to 2 hours for the subject to complete. It is usually scored by the degree of correspondence between the individual's response to the items and those of patients with various diagnoses—schizophrenic, manic depressive, psychopathic, and various categories of psychoneurosis. In other words, the test is developed around the psychiatric diagnostic schema we discussed earlier. Other scoring scales have been developed for other purposes, however. Two special methods of scoring the items also attempt to provide information on whether an individual is deliberately attempting to falsify his responses and to measure the degree to which he may be consciously or unconsciously trying to avoid revealing psychopathology to the examiner. A third special scale attempts to measure cooperativeness in following instructions in taking the test.

In general, questionnaires have several advantages. *(1)* They are easily scored and take little of the examiner's time to administer. *(2)* The scores are objective and there is no room for the examiner's bias or distortions to enter into the scoring. *(3)* The tests can generally be given to several individuals at once and can be scored by persons without specialized training. In other words, they are very economical and, consequently, they are widely used for screening purposes (that is, they are used when it is necessary to choose individuals from a large group who are in some way at the extreme of the group). For this reason such tests were used in both World War I and World War II as screening tests for maladjustment or psychological disturbance. They are also used in schools and colleges for the same purpose.

For individual clinical use, however, they have many serious limitations. The major one is that a subject may consciously or unconsciously distort his answers for specific purposes. A second limitation is that the scores obtained may provide relatively little pertinent information. Once an individual is in a clinic or a hospital as a patient, it is hardly news to discover that he is maladjusted or seriously disturbed. A third problem is that the instruments are generally oriented about specific questions that are meaningful for most people. For a particular patient, however, the questions may not be relevant to *his* problem. In other words, they do not give the patient the opportunity to describe or respond to *what is important to him.* While he may not give any indication of disturbance on the questions included in the test, he may nevertheless be quite disturbed in regard to some problems that are not included.

Frequently, this kind of instrument is used in conjunction with the trait or the disease-entity approach to personality. It is less likely to be used when the clinician is seeking information about "dynamics" or the underlying motivational basis for behavior. Some new questionnaires, such as one devised by D. Crowne and D. Marlowe[9] are being developed, however, and these do not depend on assuming the accuracy of a subject's self-report; they measure more subtle motivations. This type of test includes special items that are unlikely to be true of anyone, and the clinician can make inferences about the strength of particular needs based upon a subject's endorsement of these items. An example of one such item would be "I never feel angry no matter how unfairly I have been treated."

One illustration of the practical utility of a simple questionnaire approach to measurement is provided by a study by William Piper. For some time psychotherapists have sought a method of predicting which patients will terminate therapy after one or two sessions and before they seem to have obtained any benefits from the therapy. Such prediction is practically important because college and public clinics usually have long waiting lists and it is important not to waste the limited time of available pscyhotherapists on patients who are not motivated to stay in therapy long enough to obtain any benefit. Using social learning theory as a basis for his thinking, Piper used a revised version of the Mooney Problem Check List. He asked college students requesting psychotherapy in a mental health clinic to place checks next to brief descriptions of a great many psychological problems and symptoms if they were bothered by such problems. However, Piper requested subjects not only to check such problems but to rate each problem on whether or not they expected to be helped with this problem by psychotherapy and also to rate each problem on how important it was to him to obtain help. He used the average rating of expectancy for help and the average rating of the importance of solving the problem as measures of freedom of movement and need value, respectively. These two variables, it will be recalled, are the major determinants of goal-directed behavior in social learning theory.

He compared subjects who terminated therapy in less than four sessions (without benefit, according to their therapist) with those who remained in therapy for at least eight sessions, predicting that those who were high on both variables would be remainers and those low on both variables would be terminators. The success of his prediction is shown in Table 4.

It can be seen that, of the group from which one would expect few terminators—the high-expectancy and high-reinforcement-value group—only two out of fifteen were terminators. In the group in which one would expect few remainers—the low-expectancy and low-reinforcement-value group—only three out of thirteen were remainers. Of course, the success of this simple self-rating technique cannot be generalized to all such techniques. It does illustrate, however, that when such methods are devised for specific purposes to be used in a specific situation they can indeed be very useful.

[9] "A New Scale of Social Desirability Independent of Psychopathology," *Journal of Consulting Psychology* 24 (1960): 349–54.

Table 4

Therapy Remainers and Terminators with High and Low Expectancies and High and Low Reinforcement Value

GROUP	TOTAL N OF PATIENTS	NUMBER AND PERCENT OF REMAINERS	NUMBER AND PERCENT OF TERMINATORS
High expectancy and high reinforcement value	15	13 (87%)	2 (13%)
High expectancy and low reinforcement value	5	2 (40%)	3 (60%)
Low expectancy and high reinforcement value	7	3 (43%)	4 (57%)
Low expectancy and low reinforcement value	13	3 (23%)	10 (77%)

From William E. Piper, "The Relation of Expectancy to Several Variables Related to Psychotherapy." Master's thesis, University of Connecticut, 1969, by permission.

PROJECTIVE TECHNIQUES

Partly in an effort to avoid the limitations of self-reports and partly in an effort to get at unconscious motivations rather than surface traits and attitudes, a relatively new kind of instrument has received wide use in clinical assessment. These instruments are generally called projective techniques rather than tests because in general their administration is informal and the scoring and interpretation is more subjective. Usually a subject is asked to do some simple but imaginative task—to make some drawings, to complete some incompleted sentences, to tell stories about pictures, or to tell what kinds of associations are evoked by particular kinds of stimuli. It is assumed in these tests that what a subject produces, whether imaginative or organizational, reveals important and stable characteristics of his own personality.

There are many different kinds of projective tests; most of them have all or some of the characteristics listed below.

1. The method is indirect. Compared with the questionnaires, it is more difficult for a subject who wishes consciously to distort to know what represents a "good" versus a "bad" answer or a "right" versus a "wrong" answer. Even when he is unconsciously defensive he is not able to avoid revealing particular aspects of himself because he has no knowledge of what the examiner is seeking. Although this is not completely true of all projective techniques, it is more true of them than of questionnaires. In some instances, particularly in the case of the Rorschach Inkblot Test, the disguise of purpose has been lost for many subjects because of frequent descriptions in newspapers, popular magazines, movies, and television.

2. There is freedom of response. Freedom of response is the second important characteristic of some of the projective methods. Instead of merely being able to answer yes, no, or question mark, or to indicate the degree of agreement, it is possible to make a great variety of responses to the test task. If asked to tell a story about a picture, a hundred subjects can give a hundred different stories. In this way it is assumed that the responses of the subject reveal what is important and crucial for him. While one subject, asked to tell stories about a series of pictures, may tell stories mainly concerned with death or suicide, another given the same pictures may tell stories all concerned with achievement and success.

3. Test interpretation deals with many variables. Since it is possible for the subject to respond in many different ways, it is also possible that in interpreting the tests, many different kinds of variables can be assessed or measured. Not all subjects can be measured on the same variables, and this limits some of these instruments in their usual method of interpretation for research purposes. Although it may be possible with one subject to determine how hostile he is, and for another to what extent he is dependent on his mother for emotional satisfactions, the more variables* an instrument can potentially measure, the more difficult it is to obtain norms or objective ways of scoring the tests.

Many of the projective techniques can be scored objectively, but in so doing one loses some of the advantages. In other cases, although the scores may be arrived at objectively, the interpretation of the scores still requires a great deal of subjective judgment. As a result, the projective tests, though exceedingly valuable for clinical purposes, tend to provide hypotheses rather than "facts" about the patient. Also, extensive training and experience is required of test administrators before these instruments can be used wisely. Frequently, the tests require much more time to give, score, and interpret than do other types of personality measures. On the other hand, the trained, experienced examiner has an opportunity to observe a variety of patients in a relatively standard situation and to make judgments about how motives and less obviously important characteristics of each individual determine his behavior.

There is evidence that many situational factors influence reponses to projective tests. These too must be assessed by the experienced clinician in making his judgments. The assumption of disguise of purpose is also not always justified, as has been shown by research findings that subjects can make a better impression if they are instructed to do so. Although in many cases a subject cannot give a good impression, partly because he does not know how to, it is still clear that he will at least react very inhibitedly if he thinks the test results can be used to put him in a bad light. His test responses will be significantly different from those he gives when he feels that the test is not being used for purposes of selection.

An example of how subjects will change their way of responding in different situations is provided by a study of Edith Henry and the author.[10] In this study two groups of thirty female college students were given the Rorschach Inkblot Test. One group, the control group, received the regular instructions, which state that people see different things in the inkblots and that they are to tell the examiner what they see or what the inkblots remind them of, and that there are no right or wrong answers. The experimental group got the same instructions, but prior to that they were told—or re-minded—that the test had been used in mental hospitals for many years to study emotional disturbances and that it was being used in this experiment to make a college survey. This slight and apparently innocuous addition to the regular instructions, reminding most subjects of what most of them already knew through newspaper articles, television programs, and movies produced marked changes in the mean scores of the two groups. The aver-age total number of responses for each subject in the experimental group was 16 as compared to 23 in the control group. This was a highly significant difference. It meant that the subjects in the experimental group were much more careful in picking out things in the blots in which the form was very clear-cut. That is, they allowed themselves less freedom and imagination. The percentage of popular, or stereotyped, responses rose from 4 percent in the control group to 12 percent in the experimental group.

Not only can slight variations in instructions affect the projective test responses of subjects, but the characteristics of the examiner may also be significant. In fact, such examiner effects can be demonstrated to be signifi-cant not only for projective tests but for questionnaires and tests of ability. An example of such a study is an investigation by Paul Mussen and Alvin Scodel.[11] They presented two groups of male students with a series of eight slides of attractive nude women and asked the students to rate the attrac-tiveness of each one. Following this they were asked by another experi-menter to write stories (for a separate study) to a series of pictures from the Thematic Apperception Test (TAT). The difference between the two groups was that in one group the nude pictures were presented by a formal, profes-sorial, and somewhat stern man in his sixties and in the other group the nude slides were presented by an informal, young-looking, permissive graduate student. As expected, they found that the sexual content in the stories written to the TAT pictures was greater for the group shown the nude pictures by the informal graduate assistant.

[10] Edith Henry and J. B. Rotter, "Situational Influences on Rorschach Responses," *Journal of Consulting Psychology* 20 (1956): 457–62.

[11] Paul H. Mussen and Alvin Scodel, "The Effects of Sexual Stimulation under Varying Conditions on TAT Sexual Responsiveness," *Journal of Consulting Psychology* 19 (1955): 90.

In spite of these limitations, however, projective tests can be quite valuable in providing information not easily obtained by direct methods. A good clinician regards the judgments he makes from such tests as hypotheses to be dealt with cautiously and, if possible, checked with other kinds of data.

ILLUSTRATIONS OF PROJECTIVE TESTS

The word-association test. A forerunner of the modern projective test still used in several clinics is the word-association test. Subjects are given a stimulus word and asked to tell as quickly as possible the first word that comes to mind as an association. The clinician studies indications of mental or emotional upset revealed by long-delayed responses or other response characteristics as well as the content of the responses. The underlying basis of this test as a clinical instrument lies in the notion that thought disturbances typical of certain abnormal groups are revealed by the process of association. To this notion Jung, an early colleague of Freud's, added the idea that the association process could reveal unconscious, repressed ideas and serve as a method of discovering "unconscious complexes."

For illustrative purposes, presented below are ten responses given by a hospitalized adult male diagnosed as "schizophrenic" compared to ten common responses of "normal" adults of about the same educational level. The stimulus words are part of the Kent-Rosanoff Word Association Test.

WORD ASSOCIATION

Stimulus Word	"Normal" Responses	"Schizophrenic" Patient Responses
table	chair	chair
hand	hold	sin
smooth	rough	touch
woman	man	bad
sleep	pillow	death
stomach	eat	open
yellow	blue	fire
bed	sleep	shame
baby	girl	fire
afraid	dark	God

The Rorschach test. The Rorschach Test is one of the most widely used and known projective techniques. In this test, the subject is presented with a series of ink blots and is asked to tell what they suggest to him. There are no correct or incorrect responses, but what the subject sees in the ink blots presumably reflects his own personality. Originally, the associations were scored and interpreted in such a way that the examiner could compare a subject's responses to those of patients in different categories. The theoretical basis for scoring was that pathological types presumably tended to imagine objects in characteristically different ways. For example, images might be typically visual or kinesthetic. Faculty concepts also play an important role in Rorschach scoring, with different responses representing emotions, will, and intellect. In its current usage, other kinds of variables are assessed from the responses, including those important for the psychoanalytic study of the individual.

The thematic apperception test. In an attempt to measure the needs that are the significant variables in his theory of personality, Murray and his co-workers developed a series of tests of the projective type. Murray assumed that the subject was not usually aware of his own needs and that some instrument to reveal his unconscious thought would provide a better understanding than tests that depended on self-report. He felt that fantasy provided such a means of obtaining unconscious motives and devised a series of techniques in which the patient told his fantasies when he was listening to music, or completing incomplete stories, or when telling stories about pictures. The latter instrument, in which the subject was asked to tell a story about a picture, became the most widely used of these techniques. There is now available a standard series of pictures for clinical purposes, and also special sets of pictures to measure particular variables for both clinical and experimental purposes.

Shown in Figures 1 and 2 are pictures of the type used in such tests, but

FIGURE 1

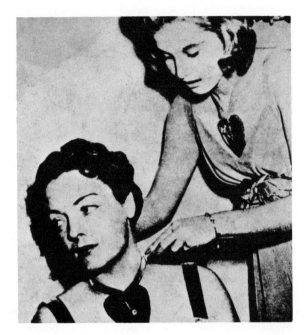

FIGURE 2

not part of any standard series; the verbatim stories told by two different young women follow. They illustrate how different these stories may be. The reader may speculate for himself about the personality of the two subjects.

FIGURE 1

Subject 1.   Well, I would say that this girl is about fourteen years old. She has always been shy and stuck pretty closely to her mother. One day, when she was walking home from school, a boy asked her to meet him later and go for a walk. She did not know what to say so she just didn't answer him and practically ran all the way home. When she got home, she asked her mother what she should have done, and her mother tried to explain to her about growing up and about boys. She seems quite disturbed about what she is hearing because she really did not want to grow up but wanted to stay a little girl all her life.

In the end she finally went out with men and married someone whom her mother suggested.

Subject 2.   This is an old picture and an old problem. This girl has watched her mother gradually drink more and more, and she finally understood what it was to be an alcoholic and why her mother sometimes stumbled and fell down and would fall asleep in the living room. She finally accused her mother of drinking and the mother is explaining in the picture that she can't help drinking. The girl asks her mother to stop because she is ashamed in front of her friends and she thinks the other kids talk about her mother behind her back, but the mother doesn't stop. Finally, the mother is taken away to an institution and when the girl grows up she leaves town and goes to another place where she is not known.

FIGURE 2

Subject 1.   These two girls are sisters and they are at a Valentine party. It is a dance and they are getting ready to go down and dance with the boys. Both of them are a little sad and they are thinking that they will not enjoy the dance. The younger sister is helping the older one. The older one is already engaged but at the dance the younger sister finds a boy that she likes very much. She is a little shy at first, but gradually she gets over her shyness, becomes engaged, and marries the boy and they have five children.

Subject 2.   This picture bothers me. I can't tell what the one girl is doing to the other. Let's say that it is two sisters and they are going out on a double date. The one sitting down is the pretty sister and the one standing up is the ugly duckling who has to wait on her pretty sister. She is fixing the pendant around her sister's neck and thinking, "I would really like to choke her." The pretty sister gets all the dates and is the popular one and the ugly sister only goes out when her pretty sister arranges a double date. The pretty one marries a wealthy man in town and goes to live in a big, beautiful house. But one day she trips going down the stairs and breaks her neck. Once the pretty sister has left the home, people begin to recognize that the ugly sister is not so ugly and she makes friends on her own and marries a poor boy who really loves her. Her husband goes to work for someone else and for several years they have a hard struggle. Finally, the husband is able to start his own business and he does well, and they become highly respected in the community.

THE INCOMPLETE SENTENCES METHOD

In the sentence completion method, the subject is asked to finish a sentence, the first word or words of which are given by the examiner. In some ways this method is related to the word-association technique, the major difference being in the length of the stimulus. Some applications of the method, however, demand only a single word or brief response. Many different types of stems are used, and incomplete sentence tests have been devised to measure a variety of variables. Some examples of different kinds of stems are given below.

I like.......................... I get angry when ....
He worried whenever .... Negroes are.....................

As in the word-association method, tendencies to block or to twist the meaning of the stimulus word may appear, and responses are categorized in a somewhat similar fashion. Even in the tests where quickness of response is encouraged, there is no attempt to measure speed of reaction, and no real pressure for *immediate* association. The response tends to provide information that the subject is willing to give, rather than information that he cannot help giving, and analysis is usually more similar to that used with the Thematic Apperception Test than to the word-association method. As in other projective devices, it is assumed that the subject reflects his own wishes, desires, fears, and attitudes in the sentences he composes, but this method differs in that the subject's production does not depend so much upon his interpretation of the standard stimulus as upon what he is able and willing to write under the test conditions.

An illustration of how such tests are used for clinical research problems is furnished by Herbert Getter and Stephen Weiss who used the Rotter Incomplete Sentences Test, a measure of college student adjustment. Getter and Weiss were interested in whether college students who made frequent visits to the college infirmary were more maladjusted psychologically than those who did not. If they did find these two were related it would not "prove" that the medical complaints were not real or serious, but it would imply that there was a reasonable possibility that individuals who made many such trips to the infirmary for minor physical complaints might be more in need of psychological help than medical help. Getter and Weiss administered the test to fifty-five fourth-semester college students in their classroom. They then traced back their complete records at the infirmary since their arrival at the college. The tests were scored by people who were unacquainted with the purpose of the study and who did not record the infirmary visits, so that the bias of the experimenter could not enter into the results. Subjects were divided at the median (middle of the distribution) of the scores on the Incomplete Sentences Blank into an adjusted and a maladjusted group. The findings of their study are presented in Table 5.

It can readily be seen in Table 5 that the less well adjusted subjects made many more visits to the infirmary in every category except external infections. Getter and Weiss felt that the reason for these extra visits was a search

Table 5

Tally of Most Frequent Reasons for Infirmary Visits

PURPOSE	ADJUSTED $N=28$	MALADJUSTED $N=27$	TOTAL
Respiratory	24	50	74
Injuries	14	44	58
Gastrointestinal	6	18	24
External infection	14	5	19
Medical excuses	5	13	18
Other	9	51	60

From Herbert Getter and Stephen D. Weiss, "The Rotter Incomplete Sentences Blank Adjustment Score as an Indicator of Somatic Complaint Frequency." Unpublished manuscript, University of Connecticut, 1967, by permission.

for dependency satisfactions—a need to be taken care of, which was not being satisfied in college for the students with the more maladjusted scores on the Incomplete Sentences Blank.

OBSERVATIONAL METHODS

Three methods of assessing personality have been described. Two of these, the informal interview and the standardized questionnaire, are partly limited in that they depend on self-report. The third, the projective technique, does not have the above limitation. However, the responses to projective tests are influenced by a large number of factors that are not easily identified, the tests themselves require a long time for analysis, and they are potentially subject to the biases of the examiner. All three methods obtain information about subjects in what might be called an artificial or somewhat unnatural situation. Some of the problems inherent in these approaches can be avoided to some extent by the use of behavioral observation techniques.

In these methods the psychologist simply attempts to observe an individual in his natural settings. With children this is sometimes done at home or on the playground. With institutionalized adults it can be done in the ward or, for instance, during occupational therapy.

Scales for rating the behavior of children have been carefully worked out, as have several scales for the rating of the behavior of hospitalized mental patients. Where the rating is made in a natural setting, it is not generally possible for the observer to hide. In the laboratory he may hide behind a one-way-vision mirror or screen, but in the naturalistic observation situations he must generally be visibly present. To what extent his presence affects the data he is obtaining is not easily determined. It is generally assumed that such an effect occurs, but since it is not possible to obtain the same data with no one present, it is extremely difficult to determine what the effect of the examiner's presence is. From the report of subjects and observers it does appear, at least to some extent, that they get used to the presence of observers they know are rating their behavior and behave naturally. Nevertheless, despite its advantages of direct observation and naturalness, this method still has its limitations in that the presence of the rater affects the behavior of the person whom he is rating.

Of course, where a single individual is involved, this method also is quite uneconomical of the examiner's time. For research purposes, however, where a number of individuals are being studied concurrently—for example, all the patients on the same ward—the method can be economical. For instance, a clinician might study many patients at the same time in order to select out of a large number a group that fits certain requirements for group psychotherapy. For another example, a therapist might observe the patients in group treatment situation in their ward so that he may better understand them or assess the effects of the therapy in a "life" setting other than the therapy situation itself.

BEHAVIORAL TESTS

Like the observational techniques just discussed, the behavioral techniques tend to rely less on the subject's self-report. However, it differs from the natural observation situation in that all the subjects are placed in the same standard test situation.* Although the behavioral test loses the advantage of the natural situation by requiring a standard situation, it does avoid one of the limitations of the observational technique. In the naturalistic observational situation one needs to be quite concerned with the adequacy (or representativeness) of the sample of observations. That is, is the time the subject is being observed typical of the usual conditions of that situation? If, for example, a patient in a five- or ten- or fifteen-minute observational period never loses his temper, can it be assumed that he is of placid temperament or merely that nothing happened to frustrate him during that short interval? Since the behavioral test provides everyone with the same situation, there is a sounder basis for comparison.

Of course, all tests measure behavior. The term behavioral test is used here to describe those instruments in which the behavior being observed in the standard test situation is the same as or similar to the behavior that the clinician is interested in predicting in the real-life situation. Instead of asking a person whether he seeks help (is dependent) when he is frustrated or blocked, instead of making an interpretation of dependency from a story he may tell, in the behavioral test the clinician *does* block or frustrate the subject and then determines on the general basis of fairly objective criteria whether he seeks help or to what extent he seeks help. Such methods of assessment were used extensively during World War II by the Office of Strategic Services, which was involved in the selection of undercover agents.

In the behavior tests, individuals may be given dull tasks to do to see how long they will persist at them in order to please the examiner. Or they might be put into a group situation where they are asked to solve a number of difficult tasks and it is necessary to cooperate with others in order to solve the tasks. Some "frustration" techniques provide insoluble tasks and then make observations of the individual's behavior as he persistently fails in his efforts. For example, one subject may give up easily and say "it's impossible," another will blame himself but point out that he could solve it if it weren't for the fact that he was up late the night before and he hasn't been well lately in any case. A third subject may become angry at the examiner and say the test is "a stupid test" and that these psychological experiments are crazy and don't "prove anything." Of course, in such testing, it is hoped that such tendencies as that of the first subject to give up easily, and that efforts. For example, one subject may give up easily and say "it's impossible," another will blame himself but point out that he could solve it if it weren't for the fact that he was up late the night before and he hasn't been well lately in any case. A third subject may become angry at the examiner and say the test is "a stupid test" and that these psychological experiments are crazy and don't "prove anything." Of course, in such testing, it is hoped that such tendencies as that of the first subject to give up easily, and that of the second subject to blame his failures on his health, and that of the third subject to become aggressive are characteristic of how these persons react to frustration in other situations.

Some of these techniques are called *unobtrusive* tests when the subject is not aware that his behavior is being observed. For example, an observer sitting in the back of a classroom could record the amount of squirming (as a measure of boredom) that went on during a regular class period, making individual comparisons, comparing the whole group under different conditions, or determining how different individuals' seat squirming behavior changed for different lecturers or different topics.

Summary

The science of personality study is still in its early phase. There are many different theories about what constitutes the important aspects of human behavior, and different terms, concepts, or constructs are used to make abstractions about the basic characteristics of people. It should be clear not only that the clinician is faced with the problem of deciding *what* to measure but also that there are extremely difficult problems involved in deciding *how* to measure. There are several different techniques or approaches to the problem of measurement or assessment of personality. Each method has its advantages and limitations. Regardless of how easily the data may be obtained, the problem of interpreting the significance and meaning of personality tests or techniques is extremely difficult and still dependent on the skill and experience of the examiner. In any case, the findings from such tests can be considered to correctly describe and allow for the prediction of an individual's future behavior only on a probabilistic basis. In general, predictions made from personality tests are less reliable than those made from tests of intelligence or ability. To a large extent this follows from the fact that with intelligence or ability measures, the individual is tested in a situation very much like the one to which predictions are made. In the personality tests, however, the testing situation is usually quite different from the real-life situation to which predictions are being made.

Personality theorists and clinical psychologists are making new gains in understanding the complexity of human behavior and the problems inherent in measurement and prediction of stable personality characteristics. Gradually, as theory improves and newer methodologies are applied to testing procedures, both greater understanding and more accurate prediction of human behavior should be possible.

Psychotherapy

chapter five

The treatment of maladjusted persons by psychological means is a third major function of the clinical psychologist. Psychotherapy, as we shall broadly define it here, is planned activity of the psychologist, the purpose of which is to accomplish changes in the individual that make his life adjustment potentially happier, more constructive, or both.

Just as there are many ways of conceiving of the basic nature of man, as we have seen in examining different personality theories, so, logically, attempts to change an individual would reflect or be determined by the therapist's particular conception of the nature of personality. In other words, there are many methods of psychotherapy, all explicitly or implicitly related to a personality theory. In the sections to follow, we shall describe some of the major approaches to psychological treatment.

Probably the earliest form of psychotherapy practiced by psychologists was child guidance—they gave advice to parents, teachers, and others, largely on a common-sense basis, on the handling or treatment of a child. With adults, something like direct suggestion was used, either in the hope that particular symptoms would disappear or that the patient would prove capable of other kinds of behavior by the exercise of will power. With the exception of the early French hypnotists and psychologists using suggestion, the first systematic approach to changing personality was that of

Sigmund Freud whose method of changing people by psychological means was clearly tied to a theory of personality. In order to understand the nature and development of psychoanalytic treatment, it is necessary to add to our earlier discussion of Freud's conceptions of the mind.

Psychoanalysis

In the development of his theory, not only did Freud divide the mind into a conscious and unconscious, but he also proposed three different systems of energies, the *id,* the *ego,* and the *superego.*

The *id* is composed of the energies directed toward the basic satisfactions of the sexual instincts and the death instincts, including those for hostile or aggressive desires. Freud believed that people are largely dominated by sexual instincts, but his conception of these differed from the common-sense notion. For Freud, the bodily satisfactions, including those pleasures involved in the stimulation of the mouth and the anus, are part of the sexual instincts. The pleasure from feeding and from elimination, as well as what we think of as adult sexuality, Freud believed, are the primary determiners of behavior. The natural response of the organism to frustration is aggressive or hostile action. A person is not aware, generally, of these instincts that make up the id but is, nevertheless, directed by them.

The *ego* comprises those instincts that have to do with self-preservation. It is through the ego that an individual learns about the environment and directs his behavior to avoid pain and punishment. Conscious, rational processes are also part of the function of the ego.

While the individual is impelled to seek satisfactions for his sexual and aggressive instincts, the very nature of civilization, according to Freud, requires that man learn to control these instincts and to satisfy them only at particular times and in particular ways, presumably so that the organization of society will not be disrupted. In the effort to control such behavior, society sets up a series of taboos and metes out severe punishment to those who do not conform. Control of aggression, early institution of toilet training, early weaning from the mother's breast, and so on, are frustrations and punishments put in the way of the satisfaction of the id impulses by society and usually directly taught to the child by his parents. As the child begins to accept and learn the necessary controls for these taboos and to feel shame when he breaks them (for example, the child who wets his pants after he has presumably been toilet trained), he is developing a *superego.* The superego arises out of the ego. It is composed of the energies of the individual directed toward the avoidance of punishment for *moral* transgressions. The superego, like the ego, may also be partly conscious and partly unconscious. The superego is the result of a child's incorporating his parents' values so that he feels guilty about moral transgressions whether or not they are discovered by others.

In Freud's conception, the three aspects of the mind—ego, id, and superego—carry on a kind of constant warfare. The id seeks its satisfactions, the ego attempts to adjust the demands of the id to the world of reality, and the superego attempts to control the impulses if they are not socially approved.

Since not only acts themselves are disapproved but thoughts or desires as well, the superego performs its work by repressing or pushing down into the unconscious unacceptable ideas and impulses. The unconscious ideas and impulses, however, seek expression in one way or another. Many of the symptoms regarded as maladjusted or pathological are seen in psychoanalysis to result from attempts of the unconscious impulses to obtain expression in disguised form. Other symptoms are actually attempts to maintain the control of these unconscious impulses. Neurotic anxiety (or a generalized fear), for example, is assumed to be a technique by which an individual warns himself that some unacceptable impulse is threatening to escape from the unconscious. Guilt is a mechanism of the superego that occurs as a result of danger to the internalized standards. Unconscious impulses and repressions express themselves in dreams and peculiar symbolic behavior.

It can be seen from this somewhat oversimplified analysis that psychopathology as viewed by Freud is largely the result of repressed unconscious impulses. In the case of so-called criminal psychopaths, it is thought that they did not develop strong superegos, and consequently, had little repression or control of their hostile and agressive instincts. Psychoanalytic therapy, which was aimed at releasing some of the unconscious impulses, is not appropriate for them, and as a group they have not been successfully treated by orthodox Freudian psychoanalysis.

Whereas Freud emphasized the roles of repressed impulses and of inadequate superego development in psychopathology, more recently a group of psychoanalysts such as Heinz Hartmann, Ernest Kris, and David Rapaport have placed greater emphasis on the ego and its role in psychic life including psychopathology. These "ego psychologists" give the ego independent status and emphasize the person's attempt to cope with reality, the integrative functions of the ego, and the degree to which the ego defends the person against punishment and failure. Such ego defenses may also distort reality in a manner characteristic of the individual and provide a basis for understanding psychopathology.

As for the other major groups of mental disorders, that is, the psychoneuroses and psychoses, psychoanalysts generally assume that powerful id impulses are being repressed and that the disorder represents either a method for the expression of the repressed impulses, a method for controlling them, or both. The problem of psychotherapy is to release these unconscious impulses, partly by weakening the superego and allowing the impulse to come under the control of the conscious ego. The impulses are regarded as instinctual and so cannot be eliminated, yet it is impossible to maintain a civilized society and have them freely expressed. Rather, the ideal of good adjustment entails the conscious understanding of his impulses by the individual and his adjustments of them to the demands of reality. These considerations were basic to the development of the psychoanalytic treatment procedure.

In order to obtain the release of these repressed impulses and allow them to come into consciousness, the atmosphere of treatment is relaxed and *permissive.* Frequently, the patient relaxes on a couch and is encouraged to say whatever he feels without fear of criticism or moralizing from the therapist. To give both the therapist and himself clues into his own unconscious thinking, the paitent is asked to relate dreams (in which unconscious impulses presumably reveal themselves in symbolic ways) or to let his mind range freely, one association leading to another, without attempting to talk about some specific thing. This latter technique is called *free association.* Sometimes patients are asked to do free association about the things that appear in their dreams. Sometimes the therapist makes interpretations or explains the meaning of what the patient has said or done so that the patient can understand his own unconscious motives.

The bringing up of the repressed or unconscious material is referred to as *catharsis. Catharsis* and *interpretation* together lead to *insight,* that is, a conscious awareness of one's own motives and the unconscious reasons behind one's behavior. When an individual has come to an awareness of his true impulses, he is presumably able to deal with them through the ego, alleviating symptoms and making a more stable adjustment. In the course of treatment, however, it is also assumed that the patient gradually begins to regard the therapist as a substitute parent *(transference);* since he is a more permissive one, this eventually leads to the weakening of the superego restrictions. The patient also "transfers" his negative feelings toward his parents to the therapist and goes through a long phase in which he does not cooperate freely in the therapeutic procedures. This negative transference, too, must be understood and explained in terms of the individual's childhood experiences and these in turn have to be explored in detail. The superego does not give up the fight easily, and in the course of treatment various techniques are instituted by the patient to avoid these attempts to expose unconscious material. The resulting treatment is a long-drawn-out affair lasting many years; frequently even then therapist and patient may still consider it unsuccessful. In brief, then, permissiveness and positive transference lead to catharis. Catharsis along with interpretation and the working through of negative transference eventually lead to insight and ego control of impulses.

Melanie Klein and Anna Freud, followers of Sigmund Freud, applied his method to the treatment of children. The major difference from adult treatment is that, instead of participating in free association and dream analysis, children express their unconscious impulses through play. While Anna Freud makes little interpretation, Melanie Klein continues to interpret to the child his behavior in a fashion similar to that in adult psychoanalysis. Here too, the technique is long and drawn out and frequently does not lead to discernible improvement.

From psychoanalytic methods of play therapy, a number of shorter techniques have evolved that put great stress on the notion of catharsis, or expression of the unconscious repressions. In such procedures, it is assumed, therapeutic benefit for a child will follow from really expressing himself through finger painting, aggressive play with dolls, breaking balloons, being allowed to smear sand and mud, and so on. Behind such methods is the belief that the core of the child's difficulties is the result of repressed hostilities that need to be expressed in order for the child to get better.

This method of treatment has led to many insights regarding hidden aspects of personality. It seems clear to many, however, that the method of treatment is too long, too inefficient, and too expensive to be used for most people. Freud and many other analysts have themselves recognized that the method is not suitable for many kinds of patients, including psychopaths, psychotics, and people with below-average intelligence.

Although many newer and shorter techniques of therapy have been worked out by followers of Sigmund Freud as well as theorists who differ drastically from him in their conception of the nature of man, almost all the methods of treatment utilize one or another of the specific techniques used by Freud—personal acceptance, permissiveness, transference, catharsis, interpretation, and insight.

The Adlerian Approach

Alfred Adler was an early colleague of Freud's who later broke with him on several important theoretical issues, and founded his own school of thought which he referred to as "individual psychology." Adler retained Freud's idea that behavior is motivated or directed toward some goal and he recognized that an individual is frequently unaware of his own motivations and the meaning or significance of his behavior. He did not, however, divide the mind into conscious and unconscious parts or into different instinctual energy systems.

What Adler objected to most in Freud's system was the emphasis on the sexual motivation as primary both in infants and adults; second, he rejected the notion that instincts themselves are determiners of behavior. At a more specific level, Adler objected to Freud's almost exclusive emphasis on the role of parents' behavior in determining the character and adjustment of the child. Adler emphasized instead what he called the dynamics of the whole family and placed far more emphasis on the importance of sibling position, sibling rivalry, and the family constellation in general. For instance, if of two children with very similar parents one was an only child and the other a middle child of three or more siblings, the two would have markedly different personalities. Adler rejected instincts as the motivators of behavior; he asserted instead that since all children are born helpless into the world, unable to feed themselves or do anything to obtain gratifications, and have to depend on others to survive, everyone develops a feeling of inadequacy or inferiority. He felt that it is a biological characteristic of man and most animals to make up for their weaknesses by compensation* and/ or overcompensation* for deficiencies. Since everyone feels inadequate or inferior, each person attempts to compensate or overcompensate for the felt weaknesses by striving for superiority, power, or strength. Each child, as a result of his own unique experiences, learns to do this in a different way depending on what he perceives around him as a means to power. The means he develops to struggle for superiority, Adler referred to as "the style of life." In the development of a neurotic or pathological style of life, Adler felt, a child misinterpreted his environment. Some examples follow:

A boy seeing a younger sister favored by their parents might decide that in order to be loved and powerful he must be like his sister by being feminine. Another child discovers, because he observes his parents quarreling all the time, that the one who shouts the loudest and longest wins the arguments; so he believes he must argue and fight for everything until he gets it. Another child feels rejected and pushed aside by his parents in favor of a sibling who displaces him, but discovers that whenever he gets sick his parents once again give him all the attention and love he had before the other children came. As a result, he develops many physical complaints and becomes a "delicate child."

Adler would say about these three children described above that they had all developed a "mistaken style of life." Seeing the world from their own unique position, without adequate experience, led them to crystallize a distorted view of the whole world. Once they had developed a given style of life they failed to learn from new experience because they interpreted all new experience along lines that they had already developed. In other words, they perceive new events in a distorted manner. Consequently, they never learn their "mistakes."

Although this is a sketchy picture of the Adlerian individual psychology, it provides enough to suggest that Adler's technique of psychotherapy would be considerably different from Freud's in several respects.

In working with adults Adlerians also try to provide a permissive atmosphere and attempt to explore thoroughly the individual's early childhood experiences, particularly those having to do with sibling rivalry, displacement of affection, pampering or rejection by the parents, the failure to learn cooperation, the failure to be taught independence and self-confidence, and attitudes toward the social role of the sexes. Having explored this early childhood, Adlerians would be likely to interpret the patient's current behavior as following from these early experiences and the mistaken style of life developed then.

Adlerians are also likely to give patients direct reassurance regarding their potentialities and capabilities. Adler saw most neurotic patients as lacking "courage." In their struggle for superiority they were afraid to fail, and their symptoms were actually defenses against failure. Getting a headache before an examination, using the excuse of a sick parent to avoid the problems of marriage, as well as many of the more bizarre and uncommon symptoms of psychosis are to Adlerians defenses, or techniques, the patient uses to set a *distance* between himself and his goal to avoid a test of his adequacy.

To overcome some of these feelings of inferiority and lack of "courage," Adlerians employ direct encouragement and reassurance. They also attempt to get an individual out of his egocentric predicament* so that he will not be inhibited by the fear of personal failure. With this purpose they interpret to the patient his lack of social feeling and the importance of developing social interest and recognizing that he has such feelings but has not given them expression.

While Freud left it to the ego to take over once insight had been arrived at, Adler attempted to direct the nature of the change more closely. For an Adlerian therapist, a successful therapy is one in which the patient is clearly more productive and more socially contributive after therapy than before.

Since the patient's difficulties frequently result from his distorted or mistaken view or as Adler would sometimes say, his "lack of common sense," the therapeutic technique tends to be quite rational. That is, Adler depended to a large extent on reason to help the patient understand his mistaken views.

In the treatment of children, Adler emphasized the treatment and re-education of parents. He particularly emphasized getting parents, teachers, and other adults who live with a child to recognize the child's need for independence, his need to feel worthwhile, and his ability to do things that others value, and the necessity for teaching the child early in life to cooperate and do things for others. If the child was seen directly for treatment purposes, he was seen only briefly, generally to encourage and to support him in efforts for constructive activities.

In one sense, Freud asked the patient to defy common sense and believe that what he considered to be simple behaviors were really expressions of mysterious unconscious forces. Adler, on the other hand, drew on social norms or the common sense of society to get the patient to see his distorted view of life. It is clear that apart from the relative effectiveness of the two approaches, Adler's is the easier task and takes less time. Adlerian therapy characteristically is shorter, tends to rely on reason, and uses encouragement and reassurance. The therapist tends to interpret more and sooner and to direct the nature of the patient's changes toward being more socially contributive.

There are many other revisions of the Freudian system, usually referred to as neo-Freudian schools. One of these, the school started by Otto Rank, will be taken up next, but most of the others, such as the schools of Karen Horney, Harry S. Sullivan, and Erich Fromm, represent some compromise between Freudian and Adlerian views, most of them being closer to Adler.

The Rankian Approach

Otto Rank was another of Freud's colleagues who broke with him and started a movement of his own. From Rank's psychoanalytic studies of individuals he came to assume a *birth trauma.* The separation of the infant from the womb, according to Rank, results in a psychological shock, or trauma, that leads him to fear further separations throughout his life. This fear of separations, or aloneness, tends to produce a dependency, or desire to cling to others, that, Rank felt, is the ultimate basis for much psychopathology or maladjustment.

Like most of the other departees from Freudian psychoanalysis, Rank objected to the primacy of sexual drive as a basic explanation of motivated behavior in human beings. He also, like Adler, tended to reject the importance of the unconscious as a storehouse of energy and the necessity of exposing unconscious impulses as a first step in psychotherapy. For Adler, this meant more direct dealing with the patient at what the psychoanalyst would call the ego level, consequently, more direct interpretation and shorter psychotherapy. Rank carried these ideas further.

It is interesting to note that when Rank came to the United States from Austria, he had considerable contact with schools of social work. His task was to advise teachers of social workers, who were working with families on relief, on how to deal with the personal problems of clients. Orthodox analysis was obviously highly inappropriate, and the major problem many of these patients faced was dependency. The social workers themselves did not have the time for extensive training in psychodynamics,* and any methods they employed would have to be suitable to the level of training and knowledge they had in this area. It is not surprising, therefore, that Rank's ideas began more and more to be directed toward a method of dealing with patients that did not involve complex analysis of unconscious motivation and past experience.

Rank asserted that delving into the past served no useful purpose but rather fixated the patient in the painful past, leaving him unable to deal with his current problems. Therefore, he rejected not only catharsis but insight into the origin of current conflicts, considering neither to be necessary or particularly helpful in accomplishing change in the client. It was also clear to Rank in dealing with highly dependent individuals, that if they became involved in the typical analytic "transference," it would be hard to break off therapy and get them to stand on their own feet. He felt that the relationship between the patient and the therapist from the very beginning should stimulate the patient toward independence.

Rank's method of therapy as it gradually evolved placed great emphasis on a discussion of the relationship between the patient and the therapist with a partial rejection by the therapist of the patient's attempts to lean on him. The focus was analysis of current problems rather than analysis of the past. Without catharsis and insight to explain why people should get better, however, Rank utilized the concept of will power, a prevalent concept in Europe at the time. In his concept, will was another human faculty explaining man's efforts toward obtaining his goals. He felt that everyone has such a capacity which, if directed into constructive channels, would allow him to make a better solution of his problems. To Rank, therefore, the purpose of therapy was to awaken the patient's *constructive will;* in so doing the therapist acted as a *counter will.* Rank's writings were translated by Jessie Taft, a social worker, who also wrote *The Dynamics of Therapy,* describing Rank's ideas and applying them to social work. She introduced the term relationship therapy to describe this method.

Rank and Taft's work apparently had some influence on Carl Rogers and on Frederick Allen, a psychiatrist who applied Rank's ideas to play therapy with children. The term "constructive will," however, was not an acceptable one in American psychology, and Allen essentially substituted the notion of creative acceptance of oneself. Such acceptance is accomplished by freeing the individual of "anxiety" and "disorganized feelings" and through a generalization of the relationship achieved by the therapist in play therapy. Allen, drawing an analogy from biology, held that the growth process involves differentiation and integration and that before psychological growth can proceed, it is necessary for a child to differentiate himself from others, particularly the adults controlling his environment.

Carl Rogers, in the Rankian tradition, accepted the general principle that therapy could proceed without an analysis of the past. Rather, in his view, therapeutic change occurs through the client's ability to solve his problems himself as he sees more deeply into them as a result of the therapist's acceptance and reflection of his feelings. Inherently, Rogers's conception still emphasizes the dependent nature of the client and the importance of his differentiating or separating himself from others. Like Rank and Allen, he explained the basis for change as the freeing of the patient's "growth potential." Later he dropped this term in favor of "self-integration" to describe the internal process that accounts for improvement as a result of therapy. Rogers carries a rejection of the importance of the past further than did the relationship therapists. He not only feels that the therapist need not explore the past for the patient's benefit, but also that the search served no useful purpose for the therapist. In fact, such a diagnostic orientation on the part of the therapist would interfere with his intuitive understanding of the patient's feelings, which he is supposed to reflect back to the patient.

Rogers feels that interpreting to the patient the meaning of his behavior tended to force the individual to regard himself from the therapist's point of view, rather than from his own. He objects to such interpretation, substituting, rather, a permissive atmosphere wherein the patient is encouraged to express himself freely. The therapist, through his *intuitive* understanding of the patient's feelings, reflects them back to the patient so that he might gain insight into them and be encouraged to explore them further. (It is not always clear how the therapist is able to interpret the patient's feelings without interpreting the content of his statements.) Gradually, the patient is expected to express his feelings more and more and to gain a better understanding of them. The natural outcome of this understanding, according to Rogers, is the integration of the self and elimination of conflicting feelings and emotions. Rogers feels that when such internal conflicts are eliminated, the patient will naturally be able to find for himself ways of making a good adjustment.

It is apparent that such a view of therapy requires more an attitude and frame of mind or particular kind of personality on the part of the therapist than it does some form of special training. Rogers's approach to therapy opens the way for people of many disciplines to engage in treament without requiring a long training program, personal analysis, or medical background. His early book, *Counseling and Psychotherapy,* published a few years before the rapid growth of clinical psychology after World War II, was widely read. Rogers also brought the psychologists' interest in research and research orientation into the field of therapy, and his published use of recorded therapy interviews opened the door to other psychologists to undertake research in this area.

One interesting side effect of the Rogerian movement is the denial of the necessity for diagnosis or even description of the individual's personal characteristics—the more a clinical psychologist accepts Rogers's orientation, the less he is concerned with or interested in diagnostic methods. In addition, the gradual disillusionment with the validity of techniques in common practice resulted in greater and greater interest in psychotherapeutic techniques, particularly in the settings where psychotherapy was possible.

Although Rogers's work led many psychologists to feel that psychotherapy was a legitimate field of application for them, they often differed strongly with Rogers's methods and his approach to personality theory.

Rogers further contributed heavily to the growth of psychotherapy through his emphasis on recorded psychotherapeutic sessions that could be studied and analyzed, and through his attempts to devise an effective method of treatment that was considerably shorter than many others. Even so, many psychologists feel that the treatment is too limited in the kinds of patients it can help significantly. Rogers's formulations both about therapy and the nature of personality also involve concepts that are difficult to measure. Consequently, it is difficult, if not impossible, to test the validity of many of his ideas.

A Social Learning Approach

One of the major contributions of American psychology has been an extensive development of learning theory. As a natural consequence, important attempts to apply learning theory to the problems of psychotherapy have been made by John Dollard and Neal Miller and by Hobart Mowrer. The learning model they used stemmed primarily from the studies of subhuman species in highly controlled, relatively simple laboratory experiments. The following section deals with the application of learning theory to psychotherapy based on the social learning theory of the author described earlier. This theory is based on research with humans in relatively complex social interactions.

From this point of view, the problems of psychotherapy are problems of how to effect changes in behavior through the interaction of one person with another. That is, they are problems in human learning in a social situation.

It will be recalled that according to social learning theory the strength (or the potential of occurrence) of goal-directed behavior depends on a person's expectancy that the behavior will lead to a desired outcome as well as on the value of that outcome for him. The likelihood for a set of related behaviors to occur in a given set of situations is called *need potential.* The expectancies that these behaviors will lead to a set of goals, reinforcements, or rewards is called *freedom of movement,* and the value importance or preference value of the reinforcements is referred to as *need value.* In order to understand, in general terms, the application of social learning theory to psychotherapy, we must examine some additional concepts.

When freedom of movement is low and need value is high—in other words, when an individual has a low expectation of obtaining certain gratifications that he desires—then defensive or maladaptive behavior frequently arises. Instead of learning how to achieve his goals, he learns how to avoid, or defend himself against, the failure and the frustration of not achieving his goals, or he may attempt to reach the goals by irreal ways.

Low freedom of movement may result from his lack of knowledge or ability to acquire adequate behaviors to reach his goals. (For example, the college boy from a small town, who greatly desires social acceptance from girls, is not shy but doesn't know the accepted manner of approach for the new social group he has joined.) Low freedom of movement may also be a consequence of the nature of the goal itself, which may frequently result in strong punishments in a specific society. (For example, some people have a strong desire to avoid responsibility and attempt to make others responsible for their actions. In order to accomplish this, they must avoid the adult role in many situations, and by so doing they frequently make people angry with them because of their need to blame others.) A mistaken expectancy for failure may result from the generalization of experiences of frustration in one life area to another. For example, a child who learns that he cannot be good in athletics because of a partial leg paralysis may generalize these feelings of inadequacy to other areas and feel that because he cannot play as well as other children, the other children do not like him. Another example would be that of a child who does poorly in school and feels, because he finds it difficult to make grades that his parents and teachers find acceptable, that the other children will likewise reject him because he is a "dumbbell."

That such generalizations take place is shown in a study by Vaughn Crandall. Crandall developed a way of measuring freedom of movement from stories told to pictures of the thematic apperception type (see Chapter 4). He developed two equivalent sets of nine pictures each to measure freedom of movement in three need areas. Each need area was represented by three pictures. One of these was recognition for physical skill (athletic coordination), one was recognition for academic skill, and the third was need for love or affection from the opposite sex. Crandall gave one set of pictures to a group of thirty male subjects and then asked them to do a series of difficult, if not impossible, coordination tasks at which they all failed. After this he gave them the second series of nine pictures in order to measure changes in freedom of movement that took place in all three need areas when the subjects were frustrated only in the need area of recognition for athletic skills. Stories were noted by judges for freedom of movement on a scale of 0 to 7. A control group of thirty-six subjects did not have the failure experience following the first set of pictures, but after spending an equal amount of time in "neutral" activity, they also told stories to the second series. Figure 3 shows the results of this study.

Note the amount of lowering of freedom of movement in the three need areas for the frustrated group as compared to the control group. Clearly the expectancy for failure as a result of frustration increased for the experimental subjects significantly in the area of recognition for physical skills. It also increased significantly, but not as much, in the somewhat related area of recognition for academic skills, and increased, but still less, in the more unrelated area of gratification from opposite-sex peers. But since the frustration was only in physical skills, the study demonstrates how expectancies for failure may generalize from one need to other needs.

Low freedom of movement may also result from "mistaken" evaluations of the present because of early experience. (For example, a girl whose sister was prettier and so was made much of by their father grows up to think of herself as "ugly" and expects that no boy could like her, though she is, in fact, an attractive girl by most standards.) In summary, then, for a given

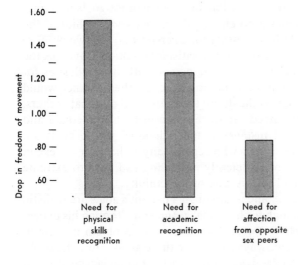

Drop in freedom of movement

1.60 —
—
1.40 —
—
1.20 —
—
1.00 —
—
.80 —
—
.60 —

Need for
physical
skills
recognition

Need for
academic
recognition

Need for
affection
from opposite
sex peers

FIGURE 3. Difference in the amount of lowering freedom of movement in Crandall's experimental subjects compared to his control subjects. (From data reported by Vaughn J. Crandall, "An Investigation of the Specificity of Reinforcement of Induced Frustration," *Journal of Social Psychology* 41 (1955): 311–18.

person, sometimes lack of knowledge of the necessary behaviors, sometimes the nature of his goals, and sometimes "erroneous" expectations are the primary source of difficulty. This concept of low freedom of movement, or anticipation of failure and punishment, overlaps to some extent with the construct of "anxiety" used in other approaches.

One important aspect of low freedom of movement relates to the concept of *minimal goal level*. In any given situation the possible outcomes of behavior can be ordered on a scale from a very high positive reinforcement, or reward, to a very high negative reinforcement, or punishment. The theoretical point at which, in this ordering, the outcome changes from positive to negative is called the minimal goal level. Such a concept can be applied either to a series of goals of the same class (for example, school grades, A, B, C, D, F) or to any combination of outcomes possible in a given situation or set of situations. An individual may have low freedom of movement, even though from the viewpoint of others he often appears to succeed, because his reinforcements are usually below his own minimal goal level. An example of high minimal goals is the student who is unhappy and upset because he has received one B grade along with three As. Another example is the girl with very high goals for social status who is ashamed to be seen with a boy who is not a member of the "best" campus fraternity. Such internalized high minimal goals are frequently involved in problems of low freedom of movement. It should be stressed that the goals can be of any kind: moral, ethical, achieving, sexual, affectional, dominating, dependent, and so on. In social learning theory, any functionally related set of reinforcements toward which an individual strives is the basis for assuming a need and for which a need potential, freedom of movement, and need value can be determined.

In order to increase a patient's freedom of movement for goals he values highly, one possible approach is to change the importance to him of the goals themselves. This might be necessary for a person who has two or more goals of high value that conflict so that the satisfaction of one involves the frustration of the other. An example is the person with strong desires for masculinity and dependency in the same situation. Another instance would be a patient whose goals, such as the desire to control and dominate others, lead to conflict with others' needs and eventuate in both immediate and delayed punishment. A third instance is the individual whose goals are unrealistically high, such as a man who regards any indication of fear in himself as proof that he is not sufficiently masculine and goes to extreme lengths to avoid any "proof" of his lack of masculinity.

As noted above, in some instances, although a patient's goals are realistic enough and appropriate enough for his social group and although his expectancies are based accurately on present situations, his problem may lie in having learned inadequate pathways to achieve these goals. Here the problem might be regarded as pedagogical. Frequently, a clinician must teach a patient the idea of searching for alternative ways of reaching goals both as a general technique of dealing with problems and as a method of achieving specific satisfactions in current life situations. The assumption that once a person is free from internal disorganization, conflict, or repression, he will automatically be able to find adequate ways to reach his goals, does not appear to be substantiated.

In predicting behavior, social learning theory emphasizes the importance of the psychological situation in addition to internal states. The individual who may be dominating, inconsiderate, and grasping for power at work, may be submissive at home and affectionate toward his family. The mild-mannered, seemingly retiring and shy professor frequently turns into a highly vocal participant and aggressive spectator at a football game. The child who has learned that he can "get away with anything at home" may be quite conforming at school, once he has learned that he will be disciplined for unacceptable behavior in that setting. Similarly, the child who gives no trouble in the warm affectionate atmosphere of the home may be sullen and hostile in a school situation where he feels he is being ignored and treated unfairly. From this point of view, personality is not merely composed of characteristics entirely within the individual; rather it is a potential to respond in a given way to a given situation. The general tendency to neglect the importance of the situation stems from the old disease-entity approach to personality, which assumed that the crucial determinant of behavior was some internal condition that would be present regardless of the specific situation in which the person found himself. The specific social situation apparently does not seriously affect the progress of measles, and it was assumed that psychic disorders or mental disorders were of a similar nature.

Two implications of emphasizing the psychological situation in determining behavior are: *(1)* that the clinician should make a greater attempt to develop the patient's understanding and discrimination* of different situations, including a better understanding of other people; and *(2)* that he should make more use of environmental control, that is, manipulations of the individual's surroundings, to effect changes in his behavior.

It can be seen from the foregoing paragraphs that there are many possibilities for changing behavior. A person can learn new behaviors or increase the potential of old behaviors in specific situations. He may learn general methods of solving problems, he may change old expectancies or change the value he places on certain goals, he may reduce his minimal goals, or he may acquire a better understanding of what behavior is appropriate for different situations.

Although it is not possible in this brief survey to describe how these different changes are accomplished, it is possible to summarize some of the major characteristics of the application of social learning theory to psychotherapy.

Since patients come into therapy with many different motives and many different past experiences, it is generally assumed that the conditions for optimal learning will vary considerably from patient to patient. One characteristic of therapy derived from a social learning point of view is that the technique must be suited to the patient. This requires the therapist to have great flexibility in his methods, since there is no single special technique that can be applied to all cases. Since it is true that some therapists are more effective with particular methods and less so with others, it is hoped that eventually patients can be matched systematically to therapists. Until then, psychotherapists will usually work with the kinds of cases and the kinds of methods with which they are most effective.

Another general characteristic of social learning theory is its problem solving orientation toward the patient's difficulties. Patients can frequently be understood in terms of their failure to meet the challenges of making an adjustment in their society and to make use of their own potentials or assets. Consequently, the theory emphasizes the development of problem-solving skills, such as those of looking for alternative ways of reaching goals, analyzing the consequences of behavior, understanding the motives of others, and trying to analyze how one situation differs from others.

Since the therapist perceives his function partly as that of guiding the learning process—not only are there inadequate behaviors and attitudes to be weakened or eliminated but also more satisfying and constructive alternatives to be learned—the tendency in social learning theory is for a highly active role on the part of the therapist. He is more active in making interpretations to patients, in directly reinforcing or rewarding particular kinds of optimal behavior, and in helping the patient find new alternatives to deal with problems. In order to do all this successfully, it is necessary that the patient trust him and accept his objectivity in the situation. Consequently, the good therapist is "warm" and communicates to his patients his concern and interest in them.

In the changing of the nature or value of life goals, the therapist must consider how these goals relate to future satisfactions. A patient may obtain gratifications in his current life from his ability to dominate a marital partner or his children but not recognize that the long-term consequences of such behavior will involve serious frustrations. One characteristic of a social learning theory is that it not only emphasizes insight into one's own motives as they have been developed from past experience, but also insight into the motives of others and insight into the long-term consequences of one's own behavior.

Finally, the therapist with a social learning orientation tends to make greater use of environmental change in order to effect personality change. In the face-to-face treatment of either children or adults, he may accomplish this by changing attitudes of others who live with the patient—by treating or occasionally consulting with marital partners, parents, or others. He may accomplish it by altering the individual's environment—by changing schools, or jobs, or play or social groups. Of course, such changes with children are usually accomplished through consultation with parents and teachers. With adults they are accomplished through direct discussion about the advisability and consequences of their making such attempts to change their own environmental conditions.

Most broadly considered, social learning theory implies that psychotherapy is a social interaction. The therapist helps the patient achieve a more satisfactory and constructive interrelationship with his social environment. The laws and principles that govern behavior in other interpersonal situations apply as well to the therapy situation.

Although the author obviously feels that social learning theory holds great promise for the future in the development of more effective and scientifically grounded approaches to psychological treatment, it should be noted that there is still much work to be done before the optimal conditions for learning for different individuals can be readily determined. Much of what social learning theory has to contribute to this field is its orientation, which points the way to future research and development.

Behavior Modification Methods

Although social learning theory implies a broad variety of therapeutic methods for psychological treatment, some rather specific methods have been devised as applications of conditioning approaches to learning. One such group of methods recently associated with Joseph Wolpe has been called relaxation or desenitization therapy.[1] Wolpe believes learned anx-

[1] Joseph Wolpe and Arnold Lazarus, *Behavior Therapy Techniques* (New York: Pergamen Press, 1966).

iety to be at the base of many neurotic problems. For Wolpe, anxiety itself or the behavior that one develops to escape the anxiety, such as compulsions, obsessions, or other symptoms, are themselves the problem rather than merely the manifestation of the problem, as the psychoanalyst believes. Wolpe's method is based on the belief that if the individual were to make responses incompatible with fear responses in the presence of the stimuli that usually provoke the anxiety response, then the learned anxiety responses and the maladjusted responses they make to reduce the fear (symptoms) would be supplanted by the newly trained incompatible responses. He calls his method *reciprocal inhibition*. Wolpe tries to determine the specific stimuli that produce the anxiety response and then by training, or drugs, to get the individual to make relaxation responses to these stimuli instead.

Another group of methods arises from the work of B. F. Skinner on instrumental conditioning. In this type of therapy the adjusted response to stimuli that previously produced a maladjusted response is taught to the individual by positive reinforcement. If the response is difficult, it is built up gradually by a technique called shaping. For example, a child who had failed to be toilet trained, although past the age when most children are trained, could be given candy just for sitting on the toilet. When the child learned to do this without fighting or struggling, he could be placed on the toilet when elimination was likely to take place involuntarily. When the child did eliminate, then he would be rewarded even more strongly with more candy and praise. Finally, the child would be rewarded in the same way for telling the parent when he had to go.

There seems to be little doubt that such methods can be very helpful in eliminating specific fears and in inducing the individual to produce specific desirable responses. In many cases, however, the problems may be too broad and diffuse for such methods and in some cases, behavior modification techniques can be useful only as part of a broader therapeutic program.

Environmental Treatment

It has been frequently noted that a change in behavior or attitude on the part of a parent may be considerably more effective in changing a child's behavior or personality than many hours of face-to-face therapy with a psychotherapist. Pedagogic case reports too are replete with examples of marked changes in the behavior of a delinquent or obstructive school child when the school sees fit to recognize some talent or to give the child a position of importance in the classroom. On the other hand, many therapists have encountered the extreme difficulty of helping a child by face-to-face treatment when he lives in an environment of continuous rejection and punishment. Any realistic discussion of therapy, therefore, must be concerned not only with the technique of face-to-face treatment but also with the practical problems involved in manipulating, changing, or controlling the environment of the patient.

For many reasons (some practical, some legal, and some traditional), it has usually been easier to effect environmental changes with children than with adults. Therefore, discussions of methods of environmental manipulation, at least aside from vocational guidance, have traditionally dealt with children. Not only are there practical limitations to what any therapist may do to control the environment of adults (for example, marital partners and bosses are frequently much harder to reach than teachers and parents), but also the characteristics the therapist is concerned with in the adult are usually more stable and have been determined by many more life experiences. It is logical, therefore, that the most effective method of treatment may vary directly with increased age. It may well be, however, that therapists have operated in this field more because of tradition than because of real limitations, and the potential for helping adults make better personality adjustments through the manipulation of others in their environment is relatively neglected. Perhaps we need more exploration in treating or dealing with marital partners and, at least in some instances, with bosses or supervisors.

THE ENVIRONMENTAL TREATMENT OF ADULTS

Some of the commonly used techniques of environmental treatment of adults are breifly noted in the following paragraphs. It must be recognized that most adults' waking lives are spent on the job. A satisfactory job situation, then, will make other frustrations more bearable. An unsatisfactory one may make minor frustrations intolerable. In our society there is considerable pressure on men and some on women to accomplish something worthwhile through their work. In striving to meet these demands, many persons may encounter serious problems. In some cases, then, helping the individual find a different kind of employment (or perhaps a job of any kind) may be a central aspect of psychological treatment. The aim, of course, is to reduce the pressure or frustration the patient is under and to provide him with a greater feeling of satisfaction, self-acceptance, or worthwhileness than is characteristic of his present circumstances.

Another type of adult environmental treatment consists of changing the attitudes of people close to the patient. What this requires is the occasional or regular treatment of marital partners or other individuals with whom the patient is closely associated. Such treatment is becoming increasingly common in mental hygiene clinics and in outpatient treatment of seriously disturbed psychotics.

Treatment in a hospital can be environmental treatment in itself. Traditionally a patient went to a hospital either to protect himself from himself, to protect society, or to obtain some specific treatment for his "disease." Like a hospital for medical illnesses, the mental hospital, it was generally assumed, provided the patient with some specific treatment. A new conception of the mental hospital is developing, however, and experimentation is underway which regards the whole hospital as a therapeutic environment. This development is leading to increased participation of patients in the running of the hospital and in their own treatment. It also involves a change in the selection, training, and activity of hospital personnel, in addition to those who are involved in specific treatments. The purpose is to make the hospital itself a therapeutic atmosphere in which the patient can develop new attitudes and new self-conceptions.

ENVIRONMENTAL TREATMENT OF CHILDREN

In the following paragraphs we shall briefly discuss some of the major forms of environmental treatment of children, indicating the clinical psychologist's major function in such procedures.

Institutionalization. Removing a child from his home and placing him in an institution is generally considered one of the most drastic forms of treatment, one to be avoided whenever there are possible alternatives. No matter how well an institution is run, it is difficult for its personnel to substitute for the family in providing the child with love, interest, and concern. In addition, in the case of a delinquent child, placement in an institution may frequently increase his feeling that society is rejecting him, that no one cares about him; consequently, his potential for further antisocial behavior may be increased. It is probable that institutions for delinquents have created far more adult criminals than they have rescued children from a career of crime

Nevertheless, there are times when the home environment is so bad, because of severe rejection or lack of concern, that it is necessary to remove the child in order to increase his chances for long-term adjustment. The chief problem for many clinical psychologists working in such institutions is to counteract the child's feeling that he has been rejected or abandoned by society.

Foster home placement. Sometimes when it is necessary to remove a child from his home, it is possible to avoid placing him in an institution by finding a good foster home where he will be warmly received. For the clinical psychologists involved in such placement, an important consideration is matching the child with the foster parents. The clinician must have a good understanding not only of the child, but also of the foster parents, their ability to tolerate certain kinds of behaviors, and their capacity to satisfy the needs of the child.

Camps and clubs.   For many children (typically those whose parents are overcritical and overrestraining, or overindulgent and oversolicitous), the deficiencies of an unhealthy home atmosphere can be compensated for, in part, by social learning acquired outside the home. Sometimes, though, the child's society or neighborhood playgroup does not satisfy this need, because the child either is fearful of joining neighborhood groups or is rejected by them. Sometimes the standards of behavior characteristic of the neighborhood groups (as in delinquent neighborhoods) do not provide adequate learning. When the home atmosphere needs to be supplemented by a healthy peer group, but one is not readily available, then it is frequently of considerable value to place the child into specially selected groups that will help him achieve acceptance by others, self-acceptance, and independence. Such groups may be particularly useful for the overprotected or overindulged child who must learn the normal give and take of living with others on an equal footing. Clubs, preschool classes, and summer camps can be of considerable direct benefit to the child. A summer camp may also give the child and parents a breathing space when there is severe conflict in the home; both gain an opportunity to change attitudes in an atmosphere free from continuous conflict. In recommending such treatment, the clinician must make sure that the child does not perceive it merely as a technique to get him out of the home and as evidence of parental rejection.

The use of the school in treatment procedures.   Next to the home the school provides the greatest influence on the child's development. Many of the characteristics of our adult society may be traced back to school training procedures. In working with problem children, a clinical psychologist, whether a part of the school system or in an independent clinic, must work closely with teachers and other school officials if he wishes both to understand the children and to help them to a better adjustment. What the school can do to help the adjustment of a child, what it sometimes does to hurt his adjustment, and how the clinical psychologist might contribute to the school is easily the subject for an extensive volume. We may only briefly mention here some of the ways the school can help a problem child.

In our society knowing that one can do things others value is necessary for any child to be happy or adjusted, and it is in the school, to a large extent, that the child will either obtain such a feeling or not obtain it. When a youngster has limited ability and is not able to obtain good grades, it is up to the individual teacher, nevertheless, to make him feel that his efforts are appreciated and that what he does is worthwhile. Sometimes this may take the form of discovering and recognizing other talents, such as artistic, cooperative, musicial, or athletic capacities. The teacher, or possibly a special adviser, can also help to satisfy the child's needs for acceptance, liking, and affection, particularly where the child's need is great because of the absence of such satisfactions in his home. It is also in school that a child learns a great deal about both competition and cooperation. The child who is afraid to compete, who withdraws from activities because of fear of failure, can be helped in school by being taught to recognize that he is still liked in spite of failure, that failure is only a step characteristic of all efforts toward accomplishment, and that progress, as well as winning, is important. As for cooperation, our society, our industries, and our families are based on the need for cooperation. The isolated child who does not have siblings near his own age and is not an active member of a neighborhood play group frequently fails to learn the necessity for cooperating with others in order to gain acceptance in our society. Children who are egocentric, overly competitive, or lacking in social acceptance, can learn the techniques and value of cooperation in school by both the regular procedures in the classroom and by special attention from the teacher and others.

The treatment of parents. From the point of view of Adlerian psychology and social learning theory, the treatment of parents is central to child therapy. Regardless of what can be done in the placement of the child in camps or clubs, of what the school can do, and of what may be accomplished in direct treatment of the child, it is extremely difficult to accomplish lasting beneficial changes in the child unless the parents' attitudes and behavior are conducive to such changes.

The attitudes and behaviors of the parents relating to the child's problem are often the result of misinformation, lack of knowledge of child raising in general, lack of knowledge about the characteristics of their own child, or lack of understanding of the relation of their behavior to the child's behavior. But parents can change their own attitudes and behavior as a result of relatively brief contacts with clinical psychologists. That is, they can accomplish significant changes in their own behavior through direct education, interpretation, or advice. Of course, considerable skill is still required in understanding where the problem lies and in conveying to the parents, in a manner which they can understand and accept, what changes are necessary.

In many cases, however, the parents' behavior is a reflection of a serious maladjustment of their own, and longer and more thorough treatment is necessary before they can make changes. Although such treatment usually begins by centering on the child's problem, it usually shifts over to the parents themselves and their problems. For example, when parents' behavior toward a child is a result of their own overly strong needs to dominate and control, or when one or both parents try to seek from the child the love lacking from a disinterested or punitive marital partner, or when a parent is seeking to obtain, through his children's efforts, the status and recognition that he failed to obtain himself, then changes in the parents' own adjustment are generally necessary before they can react differently to their children. All ranges of possible treatment from simple advice to long and extensive treatment of one or both parents are possible, and it is the clinician's job not only to carry out such treatment but also to decide how much and what kind of treatment is advisable.

Group Psychotherapy

A rapidly growing aspect of psychotherapeutic practice is the treatment of a number of individuals at the same time, usually in groups with similar problems. One of the consequences of World War II was that clinical psychologists in military establishments were asked, primarily because of lack of other personnel, to conduct group psychotherapy. Such groups were formed in prisons, convalescent centers, hospitals, and training centers. For the most part, these meetings were called "gripe sessions," because, more than anything else, it was assumed that if the patients could get rid of suppressed hostilities, by expressing them or talking them out, they would generally be less hostile to, or more understanding of, the demands of authority. Although the success of these sessions has been questioned (some observers felt they did more to increase hostilities than to dissipate them), they served to introduce many clinical psychologists into the practice of group psychotherapy. Since World War II psychologists have continued to employ this technique with both children and adults.

The advantages of group psychotherapy are twofold. One is economic. Since there are so many more people in need of psychological treatment than there are trained psychologists to treat them, handling several people in the same period of time can be of great social significance.

The second advantage of such treatment is that it may in itself be more effective for some kinds of patients. The opportunity for patients to exchange experiences with others who have similar problems, the opportunity to observe and discuss their difficulties in relating to others, and the learning of new social techniques are all possible in the group situation but difficult to attain in the individual psychotherapy session. In individual sessions, the therapist generally plays a unique role in his relationship to the patient, so that the patient's experiences with him are not typical of those with other people in real life. In most group techniques, the therapist is there to stimulate, control, interpret, structure, and so on (depending on his theoretical orientation), but the participants interact mainly with one another.

Many different kinds of patients have been treated in group therapy sessions. With the exception of groups brought together for lecture and discussion, the size of the groups ranges from three to fifteen people. Child and adolescent groups may involve play or special activities and may be composed of delinquents, asthmatics, stutterers, the overly aggressive, and the overly retiring. Not only have children of almost all kinds been brought together in group therapy, but also the mothers of children with similar problems. For adults, therapy groups have been formed with criminals, neurotics, drug addicts, alcoholics, mental patients in active treatment, mental patients preparing to leave the hospital, homosexuals—in short, patients of almost any description.

It is not possible to discuss here the great variety of techniques and concepts employed in group psychotherapy. In addition to the application of individual psychotherapy concepts such as S. R. Slavson's application of psychoanalysis and Virginia Axline's application of Carl Rogers's methods to a group situation, concepts and techniques were borrowed from many sources. J. L. Moreno's psychodrama technique, wherein patients act out different life situations, playing both themselves and the roles of significant others, and various derivatives of psychodrama are widely used. Principles of leadership and group interaction derived from sociology and social psychology have also been applied to group psychotherapy.

A variety of more or less new techniques being experimented with now might be said to be vaguely based on existential psychology. Encounter groups, sensitivity groups, marathon groups, body awareness groups, self-awareness groups, are some of the names applied to these groups, which seem to place a heavy emphasis on self-understanding, expressing one's deeper feelings in a group situation, and discovering how others really feel about one. Thus far, little data have been accumulated on the effectiveness of these techniques, but they are intended not only as therapy for the sick but as "growth" experience for the "normal," which makes it difficult to establish clear-cut criteria to determine their effectiveness.

Although the principles have not been clearly formulated, the conviction has grown that group psychotherapy provides special opportunities. No longer is it regarded as merely a mass endeavor with the same goals as individual psychotherapy. Rather, it is a special situation where a patient has the opportunity to learn group norms, where he can be rewarded for social interest and social skills, and where he can learn most effectively about others' reactions to his own social behavior.

Adjustment, Psychotherapy, and Social Values

The previous discussions have assumed that you know who should be treated by psychotherapy and what the goals of psychotherapy are. It seems clear enough that maladjusted, disturbed, or mentally ill people are sick and need treatment, and that the goal of treatment is that they should no longer be maladjusted, disturbed, or mentally ill. Although the layman seems to have no trouble in deciding who is adjusted and who is not, when one examines the problem more carefully it is no longer simple. The concept of adjustment is essentially a matter of value. That is, it involves the notions of good and bad; defining what is good, the psychologist goes on to define who needs treatment and the purpose of treatment.

Theories of behavior, personality, or abnormal psychology provide no logical or systematic way of determining the nature of maladjustment. Which behavior or which people we would call maladjusted or adjusted depends primarily on ultimate value judgments of good and bad. Each clinical psychologist must make such a value judgment for himself. Whether we consider particular persons as maladjusted—the nonconformist who has few or no friends but writes excellent poetry, the man who is caught in the illegal act of putting a slug in the subway, the apparently self-accepting homosexual, or the patient in a mental hospital who, though confused from an outsider's point of view, seems to be happy and relaxed after years of hospitalization—will depend on our basic value judgments on the nature of adjustment. Of course, there is an implication here that maladjustment represents more than a label. The judgment implies that someone should do something about it, that society or the individual clinical psychologist should make some attempt to change the judged person. Were we to assume that nobody should attempt to change someone else unless that person seeks the change, then we could get rid of the concept of maladjustment entirely and empty a large portion of our mental hospitals.

With some exceptions, psychologists (and certainly society in general) do believe that they have a responsibility to try to help people, or at least to help them discover that they would be better off with some changes. In addition to the people who seek psychological help, there are clearly many others who would benefit from it: for example, the mother who overprotects her child; the person who is a danger to himself or to others; the only child, happy as the center of attention of indulgent parents and grandparents, but heading for difficulties later in life; and the expressly miserable adult who is apparently convinced that his difficulties are physical and so seeks no psychological help. If we equate maladjustment with need for treatment, we must determine the kinds of behavior we would include in this category.

Many psychologists have avoided the problem of explicitly defining their own values. Instead, they rely on the concept of disease borrowed from medicine. By some ultimate, though undefined, criterion, specific behaviors (symptoms) or constellations of behaviors are taken as indications of disease; anyone having a specific disease, then, needs treatment. Therefore, we have the illnesses of the psychopath, the immature personality, the nervous disposition, the psychotic, the compulsive neurotic, and the rest. Diseases themselves are identified by authorities and may be found described in certain textbooks. However, clinical psychologists as a whole are depending less and less on disease concepts and becoming increasingly aware of the need to explicitly define their value commitments.

Three broadly conceived value concepts that appear to be *implicit* in the practice of psychotherapy might be called the conformity approach, the self-centered approach, and the social-centered approach.

The *conformity* criterion for adjustment implies that a man should accept the values of his culture, that he is maladjusted when he fails to accept the mores, goals, and beliefs of his society. Of course, this view does not mean that any deviation from the norm or average of others' behavior is considered maladjusted. Rather, it recognizes that a social group or society accumulates conventions and beliefs about what is good and what is bad, both in behavior and in thought. Such ideas vary from society to society. In one society it would be bad to be highly competitive, in another bad not to be competitive. Attacking maladjustment through symptoms and disease, with the purpose of eliminating the symptoms, is one form of the conformity, or "normality," approach to adjustment and the goals of treatment. It is the generally shared belief about good versus bad, held by the majority of a society or at least of its leaders, that defines both acceptable and unacceptable behavior.

Although few clinical psychologists would admit to subscribing to such a belief themselves, like others in our society, in the absence of other explicit value concepts, they may frequently rely on conformity as the criterion of adjustment.

The *self-centered* approach holds that the internal feelings of happiness, well-being, harmony, and freedom from pain and internal conflict are the criteria for adjustment. The person who feels more unhappy is more maladjusted. The behaviors, thoughts, or feelings that result in the feeling of unhappiness or lack of well-being are the maladjusted symptoms. The psychoanalytic and client-centered approaches to psychotherapy have emphasized these criteria by implication if not by overt statement.

The *social-centered* point of view stresses the social contribution of the person and his behavior. Does he contribute to the welfare of others? to society as a whole? Does he fulfill some useful function in society? The same criterion can be applied to some specific behavior. Is it, in a broad sense, contributive to the society in which the person lives? This was the emphasis of Alfred Adler in his concept of social interest. Adler felt that the problem of treatment was one of building social interest in the patient. Harry Sullivan and Hobart Mowrer have also, by implication, accepted the same value conception, Sullivan by relating adjustment to the ability to love others, and Mowrer by relating adjustment to the acceptance of social responsibility.

These different orientations toward what is good and bad (or adjusted and maladjusted) in people are not always in conflict. On the contrary, when applied, they would usually lead to similar choices. That is, in most cases the kind of person described by the society as ideal is likely to be free from serious internal conflicts and is likely to be constructive and socially contributive in his behavior. Yet the fact remains that in many cases they are not the same and the clinical psychologist cannot avoid making a decision about his own values "because it makes no difference."

Not only do social values enter into the judgment of adjustment and the goals of psychotherapy, but they may also enter into the method or technique of psychotherapy. Some psychologists have raised questions about what constitutes the moral limits of the methods the therapist may use to attempt to change the patient. In changing the patient's beliefs about himself and the world in which he lives, what restraints should be made on the therapist in influencing the patient in the direction of his own moral or ethical judgments?

Clinical psychologists, as social scientists, still need to explore more thoroughly both their own value systems and the implications of these value systems for the practice of psychotherapy.

Summary

The preceding sections have described the differences in underlying theory, method of treatment, and value orientations of clinical psychologists and others working in the field of psychotherapy. Perhaps, though, we have overly stressed some of these differences, thus providing a picture of psychological treatment with greater diversity than is actually the case. In fact, there is general agreement on many points: that the therapist should be accepting, sympathetic, and interested in his patients; that the therapist should either be free from serious distortions of his own personality, or should at least thoroughly understand his own problems and be on his guard against projecting them onto his patients; that it is advantageous for the patient to take as active a part in his own treatment as possible, not to become too dependent on the therapist, and to gain greater understanding of himself; and that the goal of therapy is to make the patient better able to cope with future problems rather than simply to eliminate the present symptoms or complaints.

Still, great differences do exist in methods, and the length, effectiveness, and course of treatment may be markedly varied depending on the therapist. Undoubtedly, many patients who persist in psychotherapy gain great benefit from it. However, many who start psychotherapy on the urging of others do not stay. One of the problems that all methods of psychotherapy have to deal with is the loss of patients who could have been helped.

It seems clear that the psychological treatment of maladjusted individuals in our society is only in its beginning stages. There are no methods that are widely accepted as correct or ideal. Treatment procedures are inefficient and in many instances probably much longer than necessary. Very little has been done to suit the particular method to the particular patient. In short, the practice of psychotherapy is a very individualistic or subjective art on the part of the therapist. This area of psychological practice is plainly in great need of scientific advance; it may well be that advances will come through a more adequate understanding of personality, how it develops, and how it changes. By making greater efforts to apply their knowledge in the fields of human learning and social interaction, psychologists are in a particularly good position to help make new contributions to the practice of psychotherapy.

The Current Status
of Clinical Psychology

chapter six

Man has produced many remarkable machines, some so complex that only relatively few people with considerable training can fully understand their workings. But man himself is far more complex than anything he has built. To understand him, to predict his behavior, or to change him in a predictable way is a challenging task of enormous magnitude. The attempt to understand man from a scientific point of view—that is, as an object of nature following natural laws—has only recently begun. Not only have the natural and physical sciences a longer history, but they also have the advantage of being able to study their subject matter under relatively controlled conditions. The effects of pressure can be noted with the effects of temperature controlled. The structure of the one-celled organism can be examined under a microscope and its growth or deterioration studied in all kinds of chemical environments. In the study of man, however, we are dealing not only with a far more complex subject but also with one that cannot be easily manipulated experimentally. Man is the object of his own scientific interest and his personal experiences limit his ability for detached study.

Another special problem in the study of man in contrast to other sciences is that psychology is a historical science, at least in part. Usually, in order to understand a physical object one has to know its current physical properties. At this time, we have not even the slightest inkling of the physical properties of past experience, but we know that all experience changes the organism. Thus, in order to understand and predict the behavior of a human being, we must know all that it is possible to know about his past experience. Since no two people have exactly the same experiences nor start with the same potential to respond equivalently to the same experiences, each person is unique, and the devising of general laws about behavior is remarkably hard. Not only does the cautious scientist find great difficulty in arriving at generalizations, but he also has even greater difficulty in testing their validity, since he must test the validity on many people but allow for the uniqueness of each at the same time.

What Is the Validity of Current Clinical Psychological Practice?

It is not surprising in light of these considerations that it is difficult to arrive at an accurate estimate of the validity of current clinical psychological practices. Although some tests may fail to do a reasonable job of predicting the behavior of experimental subjects in controlled laboratory situations, the clinician may, nevertheless, assert that in extreme cases the tests are quite adequate for predicting to broader life circumstances. On the other hand, it is not self-evident that if one is able to demonstrate the effectiveness and prediction of some tests for relatively "unimportant laboratory situations," the test would be equally useful in predicting behavior in important life situations. Hundreds of studies have tested the validity of the Rorschach test, yet it must still be said that its validity is unknown and that its usefulness depends to a large extent on the person who is using it.

It appears well established that the psychologist, with his tests of general ability, is able to make significant and important predictions on a group basis about the potential to learn academic subject matter. Still, for any given individual, many serious mistakes in prediction can be and are made if the examiner does not consider carefully all the circumstances that go into the testing situation and many other important facts about the individual. Basically, then, even when tests are fully developed and have been carefully and objectively devised, the prediction of the behavior of a single person is a subjective process depending on experience and theoretical orientation. It is also clear that many people, including psychologists, have accepted a too widespread or generalized concept of ability. Careful and accurate prediction of behavior will ultimately require the development of many more specific tests of specific abilities.

Measures of personality and diagnosis are handicapped not only by the difficulty of conceptualizing the basic variables and by the influence on test responses of the social situation of the test itself (usually greater than in ability tests), but also by the problem of finding out whether a test measures what it purports to measure. For example, take a test that presumes to measure the unconscious desire of an individual to attack others (repressed hostility); how do we find out if the test is accurate or not? We cannot ask the subject since he is not aware of his unconscious desires; and if we go to "an expert" to give a judgment or an opinion, we are accepting the very kind of data we wish to avoid by the use of a more objective test. The problem of validation of personality tests is not insoluble, but is nevertheless difficult and complex. About our personality tests in general, we can say that under some circumstances some tests seem to predict what they purport to predict better than chance. Yet even more than in the case of intelligence tests, a full understanding of the significance of responses on some measure of personality requires the subjective analysis and judgment regarding not only the test and the circumstances under which it was given, but also a great deal of other information about the subject.

How Effective Is Psychotherapy?

It should be apparent that although many people ask this question there is no answer to it. What kind of psychotherapy? With what kind of patient? By which therapist? A method may be very effective on one patient but not help another. It may be effective in the hands of one therapist but not in those of another.

Data on the effectiveness of psychotherapy often depend either on the subjective judgment of biased individuals who are interested in demonstrating that the technique that they use is effective, or on personality measures of limited or unknown validity. Undoubtedly, many patients do benefit from psychological treatment, but it is one thing to note this and another to be able to predict who will benefit and under what circumstances. Nor is it clear, when someone does benefit, whether he could have achieved the same amount of gain in adjustment or more with other methods of psychological treatment that might have been shorter or more efficient.

As the practice of clinical psychology grows and as more and more people discover its potential, the demands for the services of clinical psychologists grow even faster. It is clear that so many people are in need of some psychological help in order to lead happier and more constructive lives that there is a great demand for techniques of treatment to allow the many to be treated by the few.

In summary, there is general agreement that the effectiveness, accuracy, and value of current clinical psychological practices is limited. As an applied science it is in its infancy. A good part of the difficulty is that the science on which it depends—that is, the science of psychology, the study of human behavior—is in itself in its infancy, so what the clinical psychologist does is still largely based on subjective judgments rather than on the careful application of known laws of human behavior. Frequently, he arrives at rules and recipes first and then tries to produce a theory to justify them later. Ultimately, clinical psychologists will revise their conceptual orientation to the study of human nature many times before they achieve great accuracy in the prediction of human behavior.

Although the rules of thumb, the recipes, and the practical insights arrived at through practice represent progress and improvement over older methods, they tend to be limited; furthermore, they are frequently erroneously applied and inefficient. Folk medicine, too, sometimes stumbles on real cures, but when a full understanding of the scientific action of a particular medicine for a particular disease is lacking, practitioners tend to apply the medicine incorrectly, so sometimes it produces more harm than good. For these reasons, a clinical psychologist cannot consider himself purely as a practitioner. He has a great deal more to learn about human behavior before he can be comfortable or satisfied with his present methods of practice.

The Training of Clinical Psychologists

In light of the previous discussion, it seems appropriate that the highest degree earned by clinical psychologists is the doctorate of philosophy. In most universities, this still signifies the accomplishment of the individual as a scholar or scientist—a searcher after knowledge. The degree signifies the competence of the individual to learn and to analyze what is known rather than being a certification that the individual has mastered certain established practitioner's skills.

The heart of clinical psychology is the study of complex human behavior. The clinical psychologist who will ultimately contribute to the knowledge in his field must understand psychological theory, theory construction, and research methodology. The teaching of practical skills cannot substitute for basic knowledge in his field.

Nevertheless, the clinical psychologist, as differentiated from other psychologists, must learn what there is to be learned about the methods of practice available, and he must obtain supervised experience in using them. He must also survive a more careful screening process, since his personality and his own adjustment are important factors in his potential to practice adequately. As a consequence, the learning of practical skills both in academic and clinical settings is, in most universities, added to the basic curriculum taken by all psychologists. The average time for obtaining the Ph.D. degree is four to five years of full-time graduate study. This usually includes a year of internship spent working under careful supervision in a practical, clinical setting. When a student has completed his training he can add to the other professions working in the mental health field his unique training in theory and research.

It seems that for a long time to come clinical psychologists will be searchers for knowledge as well as practitioners and, therefore, will require long training. However, many specific skills can be taught to people without a long graduate education. The need for people to practice specific therapeutic methods—for example, behavior therapy or supportive therapy such as that used by companions for hospitalized psychotic patients—and the need for friendly counselors in the slums of our big cities, research assistants, test administrators, and other important roles can be filled by carefully selected people with much less training than is now required. In fact, clinical psychologists have begun to play an important role in the selection and training of such people.

The beginning graduate student working for a degree in clinical psychology often anticipates that he will be taught a number of remarkable, if somewhat mysterious, skills which he can then practice in order to help many others. He is frequently disappointed to discover that a great deal of time is spent in learning the basic science of psychology rather than practical skills, and that the practical skills are not as clear-cut and generally agreed upon as he had anticipated. Although in some ways this is discouraging, a good training program emphasizes that he is in a new and exciting field where he has a great opportunity to learn and to contribute to the advancement of knowledge.

From time to time the enormous complexity of studying and predicting human behavior scientifically has led some psychologists and others to give up the problem. They may try instead to seek oversimplified methods of helping without understanding, or they may assert that only intuition is possible, that scientific understanding is not. There is too much misery in the world, however, to yield to such defeatist philosophy. The difficulty of understanding and treating "physical" disease led to similar fatalistic approaches in earlier times, but the continued and patient study of biologists, physiologists, biochemists, physicians, and others ultimately led to major advances in the treatment of disease and in the understanding of how the body functions. Likewise, the careful, patient study by clinical psychologists of complex human behavior can lead to similar benefits for mankind.

Glossary

Association Areas (of the Brain). Those parts of the central cortex that do not directly control sensory or motor functions (such as hearing, vision, motor coordination) but presumably are involved in the higher mental processes.

Bias. In psychological testing and research bias refers to the influencing of test responses, interpretations, or experimental findings as a result of the conscious or unconscious attitudes of the examiner or experimenter.

Compensation. A term usually attributed to Alfred Adler. Compensation refers to the making up for a deficiency or felt inadequacy by striving for success or superiority in some other field of endeavor.

Delusions. An idea or belief that is generally held to be a gross distortion of reality and is so regarded by almost all the members of the same subculture as that of the individual who holds the belief.

Discrimination. The ability to respond selectively or differentially to two or more stimuli that were originally responded to as being similar or the same.

Egocentric Predicament. The predicament of an individual who perceives the world only in terms of how it affects him. Consequently, he is less capable of arriving at an "objective" or "social" or "normal" evaluation of people or events in his life circumstances.

Etiology. This term is used to describe the underlying basis, cause, or antecedent conditions necessary to the development of some disorder.

Form Board. An apparatus for the testing of form discrimination and eye–hand coordination; a subject is usually required to place variously shaped pieces into receptacles of the exact same shape, as quickly as possible.

Generalization. As used in therapy, refers to the carrying over of a change in attitude or behavior that arose in the therapy situation, or in relationship to the therapist, to situations or people outside the room.

Hallucination.   Sensory reactions where there is no appropriate external stimulus; for example, hearing voices, seeing visions, etc.

Involutional Period.   The period of life approximately between the ages of 38 and 55 which is usually, but not necessarily, related to a marked reduction in the activity of the reproductive glands.

Irreal.   A term devised by Kurt Lewin. Irreal behavior is directed to obtaining gratifications in a way that is not considered realistic by the society of which the individual is a member; for example, day-dreaming and peculiar symbolic actions.

Nomothetic Description.   Refers to description in which an individual is characterized in terms of his absolute or relative difference from others. It involves the use of formal or informal norms.

Norms.   The accumulation of measures of some behavior or test responses that show how members of a sample of some population are distributed in regard to the behavior or test that is being measured.

Objective.   An objective measurement, observation, or interpretation is generally considered to be independent of the specific person making it so that many individuals equivalently trained would all arrive at the same score or description.

Overcompensation.   Concept used by Alfred Adler. It refers to the making up for a felt inferiority or inadequacy by striving for superiority in the same area of endeavor as that in which the inferiority is felt.

Psychiatrist.   A person primarily concerned with mental and nervous disorders, who obtains his initial, basic training in medicine.

Psychodynamics.   The study of the underlying motivational bases of behavior.

Reification.   The treating of an abstraction as if it were something real and had an independent space–time existence.

Selection.   In psychology, selection refers to the process of determining which individuals from a larger group are most likely to fit a given criterion; for example, from a college population, selection of people who would make the best executives or selection of the individuals who are most disturbed.

Social Worker.   A professionally trained person whose main concern is helping the individual or family in their adjustment to the social community.

Standard Test Situation.   A test situation where the same procedure is used for all subjects. That is, the instructions, the order of presentation of items, and the responses made by the examiner are as similar as possible from one person to the next.

Subjective.   Subjective observations, measurements, or interpretations are those in which the methods of arriving at the judgment are not all made obvious or explicit and consequently depend to a large extent on the individual who is making the judgment.

Symbolism.   The representing of an idea, wish, or object with some other image or object, which stands for the original one.

Variable.   In psychology a term, concept, or construct that can be continuously ordered from person to person or situation to situation.

Selected Readings

Listed below are other books that will provide a different or a more detailed description of the topics covered by this volume. The general readings cover the entire field of clinical psychology and apply to all the chapters. Additional readings, particularly relevant to the content of each chapter, follow.

General

ROTTER, J. B. *Social Learning and Clinical Psychology*. Englewood Cliffs, N. J.: Prentice-Hall, Inc., 1954.

SUNDBERG, N. D., and TYLER, L. E. *Clinical Psychology*. New York: Appleton-Century-Crofts, 1962.

Chapter 1

WEBB, W. B., ed. The Profession of Psychology. New York: Holt, Rinehart & Winston, Inc., 1962.

WOLMAN, B. B., ed. *Handbook of Clinical Psychology*. New York: McGraw-Hill Book Company, 1965.

Chapter 2

ROTTER, J. B. "An Historical and Theoretical Analysis of Some Broad Trends in Clinical Psychology." In *Psychology: A Study of a Science,* S. Koch, ed., vol. 5. New York: McGraw-Hill Book Company, 1963.

Chapter 3

LOUTTIT, C. M. *Clinical Psychology of Exceptional Children.* New York: Harper & Row, Publishers, 1957.

MUSSEN, P. H. *The Psychological Development of the Child.* Englewood Cliffs, N. J. Prentice-Hall, Inc, 1963.

SARASON, S. B., and DORIS, J. *Psychological Problems in Mental Deficiency.* 4th ed., New York: Harper & Row, Publishers, 1969.

TYLER, L. E. *Tests and Measurements.* Englewood Cliffs, N. J.: Prentice-Hall, Inc., 1963.

Chapter 4

ALLPORT, G. W. *Pattern and Growth in Personality.* New York: Holt, Rinehart & Winston, Inc., 1961.

CATTELL, R. B. "Personality Theory Growing from Multivariate Research." In *Psychology: A Study of a Science,* S. Koch, ed., vol.3 New York: McGraw-Hill Book Company, 1959.

HALL, C. S. *A Primer of Freudian Psychology.* Cleveland: The World Publishing Company, 1954.

HALL, C. S., and LINDZEY, G. *Theories of Personality.* New York: John Wiley & Sons, Inc., 1957.

LAZARUS, R. S. *Personality and Adjustment.* Englewood Cliffs, N. J.: Prentice-Hall, Inc., 1963.

MAHER, B., *Principles of Psychopathology.* New York: McGraw-Hill Book Company, 1966.

MURSTEIN, B. I., *Handbook of Projective Techniques.* New York: Basic Books, Inc., Publishers, 1965.

ROTTER, J. B.; PHARES, E. J.; and CHANCE, J. eds. *Applications of a Social Learning Theory of Personality.* New York: Holt, Rinehart & Winston, Inc., in press.

Chapter 5

ADLER, A. *Social Interest: A Challenge to Mankind.* New York: The World Publishing Company, 1954.

ALLEN, F. H. *Psychotherapy With Children.* New York: W. W. Norton & Company, Inc., 1942.

GOLDSTEIN, A. P.; SECHREST, L. B.; and HELLER, R. *Psychotherapy and the Psychology of Behavior Change.* New York: John Wiley & Sons, Inc., 1966.

MUNROE, R. L. *Schools of Psychoanalytic Thought.* New York: Holt, Rinehart & Winston, Inc., Dryden Press, 1955.

RANK, O. *Will Therapy.* New York: Alfred A. Knopf, Inc., 1936.

ROGERS, C. R. *On Becoming a Person.* Boston: Houghton Mifflin Company, 1961.

ULLMAN, L., and KRASNER, L., *Case Studies in Behavior Modification.* New York: Holt, Rinehart & Winston, Inc., 1965.

Chapter 6

ROE, A., et al., eds. *Graduate Education in Psychology.* Washington, D. C.: American Psychological Assn., Inc., 1959.

Index